# THE GLORIES OF ANCIENT EGYPT
# TREASURES
# OF THE
# PHARAOHS

THE GLORIES OF ANCIENT EGYPT

# TREASURES
# OF THE
# PHARAOHS

**DELIA PEMBERTON**

**JOANN FLETCHER, Consultant**

DUNCAN BAIRD PUBLISHERS

LONDON

## TREASURES OF THE PHARAOHS
Delia Pemberton

Conceived, created and designed by
Duncan Baird Publishers Ltd
Sixth Floor
Castle House
75–76 Wells Street
London W1T 3QH

Managing Editor: Christopher Westhorp
Editor: Peter Bently
Managing Designer: Manisha Patel
Picture Researchers: Alice Gillespie and Julia Ruxton
Commissioned Maps: Garry Walton

British Library Cataloguing-in-Publication Data:
A CIP record for this book is available from the British Library

ISBN: 1-84483-048-9

10 9 8 7 6 5 4 3 2 1

Typeset in Perpetua and Optima
Colour reproduction by Scanhouse, Malaysia
Printed in China by Imago

### Notes
The abbreviations CE and BCE are used throughout this book:
CE  Common Era (the equivalent of AD)
BCE  Before the Common Era (the equivalent of BC)
Captions to pages 1–4 appear on page 224.
All measurements given in maps and diagrams are approximate.

### A note on Egyptian royal names
Ancient Egyptian kings had five titles, the last two of which were
presented in cartouches: the coronation name and the family name.
In their own time, kings were known by the first of these two names;
Ramesses II, for example, would have been called Usermaatra (his
coronation name). However, the modern practice is to use the family
name, in this case Ramesses. Confusion over names arises out of
transliteration differences that result in alternative spellings and the fact
that Egyptian kings are sometimes referred to by the classicized versions
of their names: Amenemhat as Amenemmes, Amenhotep as Amenophis,
Thutmose as Tuthmosis, and Sety as Sethos. This book uses spellings that
reflect familiar usage while remaining close to the Egyptian originals.

### DEDICATION
**In loving memory of my mother, Eileen Pemberton, 1926–2003**

# CONTENTS

# FOREWORD
## BY JOANN FLETCHER

This book tells the story of Thebes, ancient Egypt's most famous city. Better known today by its Arabic-derived name of Luxor, Thebes has been a tourist destination for more than two millennia, attracting countless visitors who came to marvel at its buildings. So numerous are Thebes' ancient monuments that the place has been justifiably described as "the world's largest open-air museum." Known to the ancient Egyptians as Waset, Thebes is situated in what was Upper Egypt in the southern part of the country. Occupying both sides of the Nile River, Thebes' population resided mostly on the east bank as what was once a small provincial town slowly developed into an increasingly cosmopolitan city that ruled an empire.

Much of Thebes' expansion, in both size and political importance, can be traced back to two of Egypt's great warrior dynasties—local families who rescued their country from civil war on two separate occasions during the 11th and 17th dynasties. As their home town became Egypt's most significant city and ultimately the country's religious capital, Thebes' local god Amun was elevated to a national deity. His cult center at Karnak, on the Nile's east bank, was embellished by succeeding generations of kings, each one eager to demonstrate his piety through increasingly generous donations. As Karnak rapidly expanded into a vast complex of shrines and chapels, its priests grew so powerful that they came to rival the pharaohs themselves—and eventually these self-styled priest-kings controlled the whole of southern Egypt.

Yet in addition to its great status as Egypt's religious capital, Thebes was also the royal burial ground for more than 500 years. The spectacular rock-cut tombs in the remote Valley of the Kings on the city's west bank once contained the mummies of ancient Egypt's most famous kings and queens, laid to rest with spectacular treasures such as those discovered in the tomb of Tutankhamun in 1922. Yet contrary to popular belief, the world's most famous graveyard has by no means given up all its secrets, and its tombs, treasures and royal mummies continue to make headlines by yielding up the most amazing discoveries. Between the Valley of the Kings and the Nile River, each king was also commemorated with his or her own ostentatious funerary (mortuary) temple. Designed to perpetuate their remembrance for eternity, these were referred to as their "Mansions of Millions of Years." Thebes' west bank plain is covered with a series of these monuments. Among the best known are Hatshepsut's terraced temple at Deir el-Bahri and the atmospheric ruins of Ramesses II's Ramesseum, the Medinet Habu complex of Ramesses III, and Amenhotep III's Colossi of Memnon. Close by lie the sprawling ruins of Amenhotep III's royal palace at Malkata, originally fronted by a mile-and-a-half wide harbor, and exemplifying the way in which this king more than any other remodeled the Theban landscape to his own specifications. A second, albeit more modest, settlement on the west bank, the village of Deir el-Medina, was once home to the workers who built the royal tombs, its remains providing a precious insight into the lives of those who actually created some of ancient Egypt's most splendid monuments.

Through a combination of authoritative text and well-chosen illustrations, Delia Pemberton explores each of these ancient monuments, as well as some of Thebes' lesser known treasures. Taking the reader back to the very beginnings of the city, she traces the way in which Thebes developed culturally and politically over the millennia, its rise and fall mirroring the fate of Egypt as a whole. She also describes the main characters in Thebes' long history, explaining how succeeding dynasties of kings stamped their own indelible mark on this sacred landscape, where the Nile's fertile banks meet the mountains and deserts beyond. A combination of history book, art catalog, guide book and reference work, written by a real expert in the field, *Treasures of the Pharaohs* is a highly accessible and attractive introduction to a city that once lay at the heart of ancient Egypt—a city whose glorious legacy continues to fascinate the modern world tens of centuries later.

# INTRODUCTION:
## HUNDRED-GATED THEBES

The spectacular monuments of ancient Thebes and the extraordinary richness of its archaeological treasures have captured the imagination of visitors to Egypt for more than two thousand years. The ancient Greeks were moved by the extent and splendor of its buildings to bestow the epithet "City of a Hundred Gates," and it was they who called it Thebes after their own famous city in Boeotia. According to one theory this name was suggested either simply by the Egyptian name of the city, "ta-Waset," or by "ta-Ipet," the name of Luxor temple. The Romans turned this temple into a military complex, which is why the Arabs called it Luxor (el-Uqsor, "the palace" or "fortress," from the Latin *castra*), the name by which the city of Thebes is known today.

The city's ancient Egyptian name of Waset or ta-Waset—"the Scepter"—was an apt one for a city that has become the symbol of the dazzling wealth and splendor of the pharaohs. From its obscure origins as a remote prehistoric settlement Thebes rose to become the most powerful city of the ancient world: the seat of kings who ruled an empire stretching from the borders of modern Turkey in the north to the fourth Nile cataract, deep in modern Sudan, in the south.

Located in the southern Nile Valley, Thebes enjoyed proximity to important caravan routes to the Red Sea and to the oases of the Western Desert. Apart

| PREDYNASTIC PERIOD 5500–3100BCE | EARLY DYNASTIC PERIOD 3100–2686BCE | OLD KINGDOM 2686–2181BCE | FIRST INTERMEDIATE PERIOD 2181–2055BCE | MIDDLE KINGDOM 2055–1650BCE | SECOND INTERMEDIATE PERIOD 1650–1550BCE |
|---|---|---|---|---|---|
| 3000BCE | | 2500 | | 2000 | 1500 |
| | 1st Dynasty 3100–2890<br>2nd Dynasty 2890–2686 | 3rd Dynasty 2686–2613<br>4th Dynasty 2613–2494<br>5th Dynasty 2494–2345<br>6th Dynasty 2345–2181 | 7th–8th Dynasties 2181–2125<br>9th–10th Dynasties 2160–2025<br>11th Dynasty (Thebes only) 2125–2055 | 11th Dynasty (all Egypt) 2055–1985<br>12th Dynasty 1985–1795<br>13th Dynasty 1795–after 1650<br>14th Dynasty 1750–1560 | 15th (Hyksos), 16th, and 17th Dynasties (concurrent) 1650–1550 |

| NEW KINGDOM 1550–1069BCE | THIRD INTERMEDIATE PERIOD 1069–747BCE | LATE PERIOD 747–332BCE | PTOLEMAIC PERIOD 332–30BCE | ROMAN PERIOD 30BCE–395CE | BYZANTINE PERIOD 395–641CE |
|---|---|---|---|---|---|
| | | All dates before 690BCE are approximate | | | |

| | 1000 | 500 | BCE | CE | 500CE |
|---|---|---|---|---|---|

| 8th Dynasty 1550–1295 9th Dynasty 1295–1186 0th Dynasty 1186–1069 | 21st Dynasty 1069–945 22nd Dynasty 945–715 23rd Dynasty 818–715 24th Dynasty 727–715 | 25th Dynasty (Kushite) 747–656 26th Dynasty 664–525 27th Dynasty (First Persian Period) 525–404 28th Dynasty 404–399 29th Dynasty 399–380 30th Dynasty 380–343 Second Persian Period 343–332 | Macedonian Dynasty 332–305 Ptolemaic Dynasty 305–30 | | |

**ABOVE**
An aerial view of the Theban
necropolis on the west bank
of the Nile. The foreground is
dominated by the mortuary
temple of Ramesses II, better
known as the Ramesseum; the
temple of Hatshepsut is visible
at top right.

from this, however, it had no special strategic importance, and its rise to prominence was largely a matter of historical accident: at two critical periods of ancient Egypt's history, ruling families from the Theban area were able to restore order and reunite the country. Under their rule, the local deity of Thebes, Amun, rose to become one of the principal gods of the Egyptian state, and his cult center at Thebes assumed the status of a major national shrine.

Modern development makes it difficult to estimate the true size of ancient Thebes. Writing in the first century BCE, Diodorus Siculus estimated that the city perimeter measured 140 *stadia* (about 16 miles or 26 km), making its area roughly 16 sq miles or 41 sq km: this included inhabited areas and arable land, but not the extensive cemeteries, which cover perhaps another 3 sq miles (8 sq km).

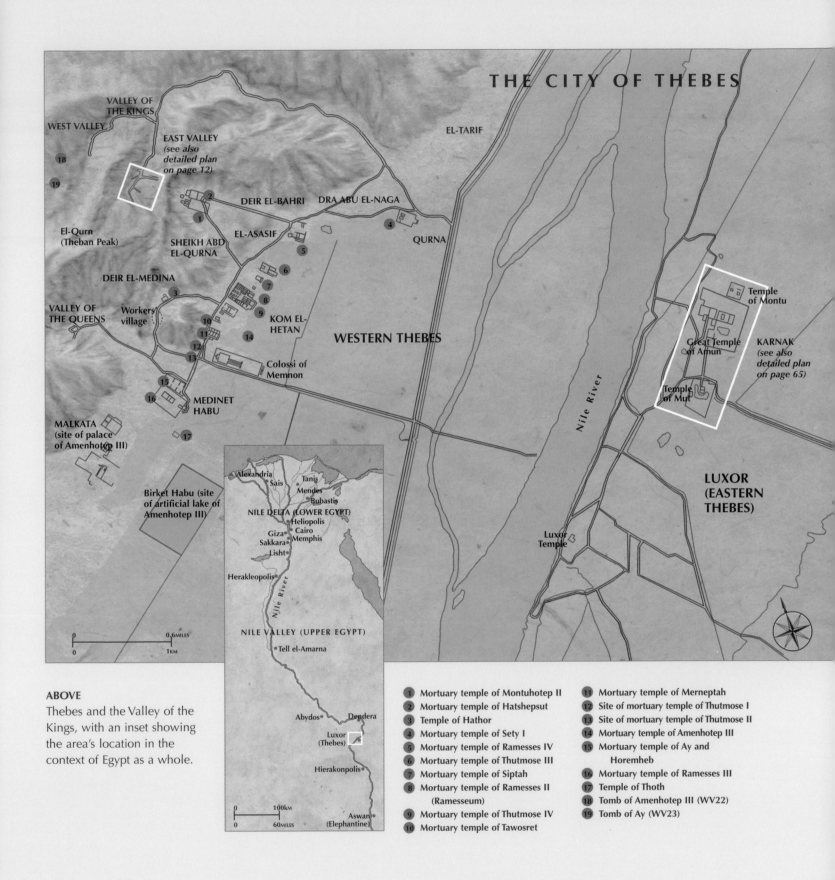

# THE CITY OF THEBES

VALLEY OF THE KINGS

WEST VALLEY

EL-TARIF

EAST VALLEY
(see also detailed plan on page 12)

18

19

2

DEIR EL-BAHRI

DRA ABU EL-NAGA

El-Qurn
(Theban Peak)

1

4

SHEIKH ABD
EL-QURNA

EL-ASASIF

QURNA

5

DEIR EL-MEDINA

6

Temple
of Montu

3

7

VALLEY OF
THE QUEENS

8

Workers'
village

9

KOM EL-
HETAN

WESTERN THEBES

Great Temple
of Amun

KARNAK
(see also detailed plan on page 65)

10

11

14

12

Temple
of Mut

13

Colossi of
Memnon

Nile River

15

16

MEDINET
HABU

LUXOR
(EASTERN
THEBES)

MALKATA
(site of palace
of Amenhotep III)

17

Birket Habu (site
of artificial lake of
Amenhotep III)

Alexandria
Sais
Tanis
Mendes
Bubastis

NILE DELTA (LOWER EGYPT)

Heliopolis
Giza • Cairo
Sakkara • Memphis
Lisht

Herakleopolis

Luxor
Temple

Nile River

NILE VALLEY (UPPER EGYPT)

0          0,6 MILES
0          1 KM

Tell el-Amarna

## ABOVE

Thebes and the Valley of the
Kings, with an inset showing
the area's location in the
context of Egypt as a whole.

Abydos • Dendera

Luxor
(Thebes)

Hierakonpolis

0          100 KM
0          60 MILES

Aswan
(Elephantine)

1 Mortuary temple of Montuhotep II
2 Mortuary temple of Hatshepsut
3 Temple of Hathor
4 Mortuary temple of Sety I
5 Mortuary temple of Ramesses IV
6 Mortuary temple of Thutmose III
7 Mortuary temple of Siptah
8 Mortuary temple of Ramesses II
   (Ramesseum)
9 Mortuary temple of Thutmose IV
10 Mortuary temple of Tawosret

11 Mortuary temple of Merneptah
12 Site of mortuary temple of Thutmose I
13 Site of mortuary temple of Thutmose II
14 Mortuary temple of Amenhotep III
15 Mortuary temple of Ay and
   Horemheb
16 Mortuary temple of Ramesses III
17 Temple of Thoth
18 Tomb of Amenhotep III (WV22)
19 Tomb of Ay (WV23)

**ABOVE**

A map of the East Valley of the Valley of the Kings, where the majority of the 62 royal tombs so far identified are located.

**KEY**

KV indicates "Kings' Valley" (that is, the East Valley of the Valley of the Kings, also called Wadi Biban el-Muluk, "the Valley of the Tombs of the Kings"). WV is "West Valley," the western branch of the Valley of the Kings.

KV1 Ramesses VII
KV2 Ramesses IV
KV3 Son of Ramesses III
KV4 Ramesses XI
KV5 Sons of Ramesses II
KV6 Ramesses IX

KV7 Ramesses II
KV8 Merneptah
KV9 Ramesses V and Ramesses VI
KV10 Amenmesse
KV11 Ramesses III
KV12 Unknown, 18th Dynasty
KV13 Bay (royal chancellor)
KV14 Tawosret/Sethnakht
KV15 Sety II
KV16 Ramesses I
KV17 Sety I
KV18 Ramesses X
KV19 Prince Montuherkhepshef
KV20 Thutmose I and Hatshepsut
KV21 Two 18th-Dynasty queens
WV22 (KV22) Amenhotep III
WV23 (KV23) Ay
WV24 (KV24) Unknown, 18th Dynasty
WV25 (KV25) Unknown, 18th Dynasty
KV26 Unknown, 18th Dynasty
KV27 Unknown, 18th Dynasty

KV28 Unknown, 18th Dynasty
KV29 Unknown, 18th Dynasty
KV30 Unknown, 18th Dynasty
KV31 Unknown, 18th Dynasty
KV32 Tia'a (wife of Amenhotep II and mother of Thutmose IV)
KV33 Unknown
KV34 Thutmose III
KV35 Amenhotep II
KV36 Maiherpri (royal fanbearer)
KV37 Unknown
KV38 Thutmose I [also KV20]
KV39 Amenhotep I?
KV40 Unknown, 18th Dynasty
KV41 Unknown, 18th Dynasty
KV42 Hatshepshut-Meryet-Ra (wife of Thutmose III)
KV43 Thutmose IV
KV44 Unknown, 18th Dynasty
KV45 Userhet ("Overseer of Fields of Amun")

KV46 Yuya and Thuya (parents of Queen Tiye, wife of Amenhotep III)
KV47 Siptah
KV48 Amenemopet (vizier and mayor of Thebes)
KV49 Unknown, 18th Dynasty
KV50 Unknown
KV51 Unknown, 18th Dynasty
KV52 Unknown, 18th Dynasty
KV53 Unknown, 18th Dynasty
KV54 Tutankhamun cache
KV55 Tye? Akhenaten?
KV56 Unknown, 18th Dynasty
KV57 Horemheb
KV58 Unknown, 18th Dynasty
KV59 Unknown, 18th Dynasty
KV60 Satra, called In (royal nurse)?
KV61 Unknown, 18th Dynasty
KV62 Tutankhamun
WV A (KVA) Unknown
KV F Unknown

Thebes enjoyed its greatest renown during the Middle Kingdom and
the New Kingdom (*c*.2055–1069BCE), but its religious significance ensured that it
retained its importance for many centuries. The great temple of Amun at Karnak, for
example, was an active center of worship from at least the Middle Kingdom to well
into the Roman period, when Thebes was already a tourist destination for travelers
from the Mediterranean world.

Then, as now, visitors came to Thebes to marvel at the magnificent
temples of the gods, the vast royal tombs, and the smaller but no less impressive private
monuments, while paintings, sculptures, jewelry, and funerary artifacts from Thebes
grace museums around the world. The significance of Thebes has been recognized by
its adoption as a UNESCO World Heritage Site, and archaeological excavation and
research continue to reveal new discoveries, adding to our knowledge and
understanding of life—and death—in ancient Egypt.

# ORIGINS

**THE PALEOLITHIC PERIOD TO THE 17TH DYNASTY** (c.100,000–c.1550BCE)

# THE WOMB OF THE GODDESS
## THE PALEOLITHIC PERIOD TO THE EARLY DYNASTIC
## PERIOD (c.100,000–c.2686BCE)

The first known inhabitants of the Theban region were clans of nomadic hunter-gatherers who, from at least c.100,000BCE, lived among the hills fringing the desert. In paleolithic times, the desert was a far more hospitable place than now, for it was a savannah-like environment rich in plants and game, while the wadis to the east and west of the Nile River were still occasional watercourses, periodically scoured by floods that created oases of vegetation and exposed flints for toolmaking.

By neolithic times, from c.5000BCE, climate changes caused by the recession of the polar ice at the end of the last ice age had led to increasingly arid conditions in the desert. Despite the dangers of the Nile's annual inundation (which no longer occurs owing to the Aswan dams), early settlers began to leave the safety of the hills for the river's lush floodplain. Once there, they soon learned to exploit the yearly flood for growing food, marking the shift to a predominantly agricultural economy.

Little is known of early religious practices in Egypt, but it is likely that each settlement had its own deity, often venerated in the form of an animal. With the passage of time, these deities became the gods and goddesses of the Egyptian pantheon: rock drawings of cattle found in the Valley of the Queens on the Nile's west bank at Thebes may relate to a cult later incorporated into that of the cow-goddess Hathor.

From c.4000BCE, southern Egyptian burials often included grave goods, indicating a growing belief in an afterlife. As elsewhere in Egypt, the Theban cemeteries were located in the desert to the west of the city, so the souls of the dead could follow the setting sun into the underworld, in the hope of sharing in the sun's rebirth each morning; the sharp distinction between the desert and the lush arable land of the Nile floodplain underlined the separation of the domains of the living and the dead.

The settled lifestyle demanded by farming fostered simple industries such as pottery and stoneworking, leading to increased social complexity. Above all, agriculture required farmers to cooperate over the storage and distribution of water for irrigation, and this led in turn to the beginnings of local government and the emergence

of small states. There were probably several prehistoric settlements in the Theban area—most notably at el-Tarif and at Gebelein and Armant to the south. However, these were all overshadowed by the powerful centers of Hierakonpolis further south and Naqada to the north, which commanded access to the Wadi Hammamat, the principal route for Red Sea trade and the gold mines of the Eastern Desert.

For the Egyptians, the most significant event in their history occurred in *c.*3100BCE, when a coalition of southern Egyptian states established control of the whole of Egypt, from the Mediterranean coast to the first Nile cataract at modern Aswan. This symbolic unification of the "Two Lands" of the Nile Valley (Upper Egypt) and the Nile Delta (Lower Egypt) was to have a profound and enduring influence on Egyptian concepts of national identity and the role of the kingship.

Unification was attributed to a legendary figure known as Menes, which can be translated as "Founder." A national capital was established at Memphis, close to the junction of Valley and Delta, and from this time the ruler of Egypt assumed a semidivine status. He bore the titles "King of Upper and Lower Egypt" and "Lord of the Two Lands," and wore the Double Crown symbolizing the union of the Valley and Delta. Above all, he became the defender of Egypt and the upholder of divine order.

The Egyptians looked back to the time of unification as a golden age, and in later times adopted a consciously archaizing approach in their art, architecture, and social organization. The older an object or institution, the more venerable its status.

**ABOVE**
A view of the hills and cliffs of Western Thebes, from Deir el-Medina (far left) to Dra Abu el-Naga (far right). The area, which was of sacred significance from prehistoric times, is dominated by the Theban Peak (el-Qurn) at top left. In the middle foreground, on the edge of the cultivation, are the remains of the royal mortuary temples of the New Kingdom. The temple of Ramesses II (the Ramesseum) is just off center, before the hill named Sheikh Abd el-Qurna; behind this, to the right, is Deir el-Bahri, a bay in the cliffs that is the site of the temples of Montuhotep II and Hatshepsut. On the far side of the cliffs at this point is the Valley of the Kings (see page 18).

# SHE WHO LOVES SILENCE
## THE 3RD TO 10TH DYNASTIES (C.2686–C.2125 BCE)

During the Old Kingdom (3rd–6th Dynasties, c.2686–c.2181BCE) Memphis was the national capital, while Thebes remained a relatively obscure provincial outpost. For administrative purposes Egypt was divided into "nomes," or provinces, each overseen by a governor. Thebes (Waset), the fourth nome of Upper Egypt, extended roughly from Gebelein in the south to Medamud in the north, a distance of approximately 25 miles (40 km).

A number of tombs built for Old Kingdom provincial administrators have been found at Thebes. The earliest of these—two freestanding, rectangular, brick mastaba tombs at el-Tarif—date from the 3rd or 4th Dynasty. From the 5th Dynasty onward, local officials were buried in tombs cut into the nearby cliffs, where tomb carvings and stelae record their names and rank. It is also possible that the earliest monuments at the sacred site of Karnak may have dated from this time.

The collapse of centralized government at the end of the Old Kingdom saw many local officials leave Memphis and return to their native towns, where they could best exploit political conditions to their advantage as rival factions jostled for power. In the north, the 7th and 8th Dynasties, ruling from Memphis, were succeeded by the 9th and 10th Dynasties, who controlled the north of Egypt from Herakleopolis in the northern Nile Valley. In the south, the Thebans were among the provincial factions engaged in the struggle to dominate the region.

It was during this period of national disunity, known as the First Intermediate Period (c.2181–c.2055BCE), that a family from Armant, on the west bank of the Nile nearly 6 miles (9km) southwest of Luxor, first came to prominence. With the family's rise, Thebes began its long climb toward national supremacy.

**ABOVE**
A relief of Old Kingdom rulers from the Jubilee temple of Thuthmose III at Karnak. These figures may have been carved to commemorate the first kings to build at Karnak.

**OPPOSITE**
A view of the Valley of the Kings (the East Valley) looking southeast across the hills and New Kingdom temples of Western Thebes toward the Nile floodplain. The earliest Theban tombs were close to Dra Abu el-Naga, which is on the edge of the floodplain on the far left of this photograph.

# THE CITY OF THE SCEPTER
## THE 11TH DYNASTY (c.2125–c.1985 BCE)

The first rulers of the Theban 11th Dynasty were roughly contemporary with their main rivals, the Herakleopolitan kings of the 9th and 10th Dynasties. Despite the fact that they controlled only a small area of southern Egypt, the Thebans clearly viewed themselves as monarchs, assuming royal titles and writing their names inside the cartouches (oval rings) indicating kingship.

The ruler later acknowledged as the founder of the 11th Dynasty was Montuhotep, the nomarch (provincial governor) of Thebes, who lived c.2119BCE. His name, which translates as "Montu is content," reflects his family's allegiance to Montu, the Theban god of war, whose cult center was at their native city of Armant. Many later rulers of the dynasty adopted the same name, perhaps reflecting their warlike and expansionist aspirations as well as a desire to link themselves with the dynastic founder.

Montuhotep was succeeded by three kings called Inyotef, all of whom were buried at el-Tarif. The limited amount of building land available on the Theban west bank made the construction of free-standing monuments such as pyramids impractical, and a new type of rock-cut tomb – known as a *saff* tomb – was developed for the burials of these rulers. Cut into the limestone cliffs, a *saff* tomb consisted of a pillared façade leading to corridors with burial shafts for the king and close family members.

Stelae and inscriptions from both royal and private monuments in southern Egypt chart the Theban ascendancy under Montuhotep's successors. By the end of Inyotef II's long reign (c.2112–2063BCE), the Thebans had established their dominion over the region from Abydos to the north as far south as the first Nile cataract. Their northward expansion inevitably brought them into conflict with provinces loyal to the 10th-Dynasty rulers of Herakleopolis, and eventually with the Herakleopolitans themselves.

By c.2055BCE, the Thebans had defeated the 10th Dynasty and extended their control over the whole of Egypt. Their first task was to repair the social and economic damage caused by the disruption of the previous century and a half. During

**RIGHT**
A painted sandstone statue of King Nebhepetre Montuhotep II wearing the red crown of Lower Egypt, from his tomb complex at Deir el-Bahri, western Thebes. The king is portrayed as the god Osiris, the mythical first king of Egypt, who after being slain was briefly revived to conceive his successor, Horus, before descending into the underworld to become the ruler of the dead. As such, Osiris was also responsible for the fertility of the soil and the growth of crops. The myth reflects the agricultural cycle, in which each year's crop is cut down to provide both sustenance for the population and seed for the next sowing. Osiris was commonly represented with skin colored either black, like the fertile alluvial soil of Egypt, or green, the color of new growth.

the First Intermediate Period, Egypt had lost its dominance over its southern neighbor, Nubia, and hence the wealth gained from African trade, while the Nile Delta had been left vulnerable to invasion. Disputes over water distribution had led to inefficient farming and food shortages, and lawlessness and crime were rife.

The last three kings of the 11th Dynasty all bore the name Montuhotep. It was Montuhotep II (c.2055–2004BCE) who finally overthrew the 10th Dynasty and began the work of securing Egypt's borders by mounting military campaigns against the Libyans to the west and the Sinai Bedouin to the east. His work was continued by his successors, Montuhotep III and Montuhotep IV, who rebuilt and strengthened a chain of fortresses in the eastern Delta that guarded Egypt from invasions from Sinai, Palestine, and Syria, and restored some of Egypt's former authority in Nubia.

The reunification of Egypt under Montuhotep II marks the beginning of the period known as the Middle Kingdom (c.2055–c.1650BCE). Under his patronage, Thebes was transformed into a great city, a fitting capital for Egypt, and the earliest known example of a town laid out on a single axis. On the east bank of the Nile, beside his palace at Karnak, Montuhotep II commissioned a great temple dedicated to the local god, Amun, who was worshiped with his consort Mut and their son, the moon god Khonsu. Before this time, Amun had been a little-known creator deity, but the rise of the Thebans to the status of national rulers saw the beginning of his transformation into one of the principal gods of the Egyptian state.

At Deir el-Bahri, 3 miles (5 km) away across the Nile, Montuhotep built his extraordinary funerary complex. Its setting—a dramatic bay in the limestone cliffs of the Theban west bank—was clearly chosen for its visual impact, while its location directly opposite Karnak underlined the connection between the king's religious roles in life and death. Montuhotep's monument combined the royal tomb with a funerary temple, where the cult of the dead king was celebrated. It was a unique design that drew together elements of the earlier *saff* tombs, such as the underground burial chamber and

A milking scene on the
limestone sarcophagus of
Kawit, one of Montuhotep II's
wives buried near him at Deir
el-Bahri. The cow has a tear
in its eye: Egyptians apparently
believed that cows wept to
lose milk intended for their
calves. The calf is tied to the
cow's foreleg.

pillared facade, with the central monumental structure and ramped causeway found in the royal pyramid tombs of the cemeteries of Memphis, the old northern capital of Egypt. This design may in itself have been a reference to Montuhotep II's conquest of the north and the assimilation of earlier royal traditions.

The tomb complex faced east, to enable Montuhotep to participate in the daily rebirth of the sun, and was surrounded by gardens with ornamental trees including sycamore, figs, and tamarisks. Beside the causeway, a hidden cenotaph, or dummy tomb, contained a painted stone statue of Montuhotep in the form of the god Osiris (see page 21). By the Middle Kingdom, the deceased king had become strongly identified with Osiris, the mythological first king of Egypt, who was said to have become the ruler of the Underworld after being murdered by his brother Seth, the god of disorder. Through the magic of his wife, the goddess Isis, Osiris had posthumously fathered Horus, who succeeded him as king. The living king, the protector and

**RIGHT**
A painted sandstone statue of the 11th-dynasty Theban general Antef, who served as chancellor and overseer of Montuhotep II's troops. The extent of his tomb, its paintings and its proximity to that of Montuhotep II himself, all serve to confirm that Antef's position at court was a privileged one.

sustainer of his people, was therefore regarded as the incarnation of Horus, and upon his death he was transformed into Osiris.

Like earlier royal monuments, Montuhotep II's funerary complex contained burial places for his wives and children. Only one queen at a time enjoyed the title and privileges of Chief Royal Wife, but the king could have any number of lesser wives, and a large number of women were buried within the precincts of Montuhotep's great monument. Two such tombs belonged to the queens Tem and Neferu (also his sister), who seem to have been his principal wives. Another may have been intended for his eldest son, Inyotef, who did not survive to succeed his father. In addition to other tombs in the temple courtyard, a row of six funerary chapels with underground burial chambers appears to have been intended to provide Montuhotep with a harem for the afterlife, although one tomb is that of a child. Artifacts found in the tombs include linen clothes, fragments of wall paintings and reliefs, and the beautifully carved sarcophagi of two royal women named Ashait and Kawit, which are decorated with scenes of court life.

From the earliest times, commoners sought to be buried close to the king in the hope of sharing in his divine afterlife. Permission to build a tomb in the royal cemetery was a mark of high social status, a privilege normally restricted to the royal family and high officials. Early private tombs of the 11th Dynasty are found close to the royal tombs at el-Tarif, but with the construction of Montuhotep II's funerary complex, Deir el-Bahri became the favored location. One of the most interesting burials there contained the remains of some 60 men who had clearly been slain in battle and buried in haste; they were very likely soldiers killed in Montuhotep's struggle for reunification.

Hewn into the solid rock of the cliffs to the north and south of the royal complex were the tombs of Montuhotep's officials. Originally these tombs were

decorated with elaborate painted reliefs of agricultural and domestic scenes that were intended to ensure that the tomb owners retained their privileged lifestyle in the next world. Over the centuries virtually all the reliefs have been destroyed, but other treasures from these private tombs have survived, including the magnificent limestone sarcophagus of the vizier (chief minister) Dagi, painted with offerings and texts to assist the deceased in the afterlife. From the tomb of Ipi, another vizier, an archive of correspondence belonging to a mortuary priest named Heqanakht gives a lively account of everyday life. The best-known private tomb, however, is that of the chancellor Meketra, in which an extraordinary collection of wooden models was found hidden under the floor of the burial chamber. The equivalent of the lost paintings in other tombs, these models re-create in meticulous detail the estate of a Middle Kingdom nobleman, from his house with its workshops, stables, and kitchens, to his servants, boats, and livestock.

**ABOVE AND OPPOSITE**
The lively painted wooden models found in the tomb of Meketra at Deir el-Bahri give a vivid picture of life on a nobleman's estate. **ABOVE** Sitting beneath a canopy, Meketra presides over the counting of his livestock. **OPPOSITE** A woman bearing a live duck in one hand and a basket containing jars of beer on her head—sustenance for Meketra's spirit.

# AMUN THE MIGHTY
## THE 12TH DYNASTY (c.1985–c.1795 BCE)

Under the kings of the 12th Dynasty, Thebes once again took second place to a new capital city situated in the northern Nile Valley, close to modern Lisht. The decision to move the capital was made by Amenemhat I (c.1985–c.1955 BCE), the first king of the dynasty. Amenemhat seems to have been the vizier of Montuhotep IV, the last ruler of the 11th Dynasty, but how he came to the throne is unclear. If Montuhotep had no living heir, he may have nominated Amenemhat as his successor; alternatively, Amenemhat may have instituted a coup.

The name of the new capital, Amenemhat-Itjtawy, can be translated as "Amenemhat takes control of the Two Lands," and expresses Amenemhat I's determination to make a clear break with the past. In ancient times, he enjoyed the reputation of having finally restored order to Egypt, thanks in part to propaganda texts such as *The Prophecy of Neferti*, which purports to be a prophecy written during the Old Kingdom but was in fact composed around Amenemhat's time or later. In it, a priest called Neferti describes the chaos that will befall Egypt with the collapse of the Old Kingdom, but also predicts the coming of Amenemhat, the one who will restore order: "Behold, a king will come from the south, and his name will be Ameny [Amenemhat]…. He will receive the White Crown, he will protect the Red Crown. He will unite the Two Powers…. Those who were disposed to evil and meditated aggression will be silent out of fear of him…. Righteousness will be restored, and iniquity will be cast out."

Notwithstanding this type of propaganda, it does seem to be true that Amenemhat ended territorial disputes within Egypt and laid the foundation of its future prosperity by reestablishing the boundaries of the provinces and ensuring the fair distribution of water for farming. He also took care to install loyal officials in key positions throughout the country. In the south, he appointed a new governor at Aswan, and built a fortress in Nubia to regain control over African trade.

Amenemhat's name can be translated as "Amun is foremost," and it was under the kings of the 12th Dynasty that Amun made the transition from local Theban

**ABOVE**
A pillar from Senusret I's Jubilee temple at Karnak, showing the king embraced by the creator god Ptah.

**OPPOSITE**
The fine reliefs on the White Chapel of Senusret I owe their excellent state of preservation to the fact this elegant shrine was dismantled by Amenhotep III and used as in-fill for the 3rd Pylon at Karnak. The scene in the foreground shows the king before the ithyphallic fertility god Amun-Min.

deity to the chief god of the Egyptian state. Although the court was now based in the north, Amun's cult center at Thebes was not neglected, and an extensive schedule of temple building was initiated at Karnak.

After 30 years on the throne, Amenemhat was assassinated, apparently the victim of a palace plot. He was succeeded by his son, Senusret I (*c*.1965–1920BCE), who carried on his father's work, building more fortresses in Nubia and mounting campaigns against the Libyans. In the east, however, he cultivated trade and diplomatic relations with the city-states of Syria-Palestine.

At Karnak, Senusret (also known as Sesostris, the Greek verion of his name) celebrated Amun's new status with a splendid new temple. Middle Kingdom temples were built mainly of mudbrick with only a few stone elements, and as a result little now remains of Senusret's structure, which was dismantled to provide materials for later monuments. However, an exquisite chapel of white limestone has been reassembled in Karnak's open-air museum. Known as the White Chapel, this shrine was probably a way-station used during religious processions, when priests carried images of the temple deities in models of ceremonial boats. A simple colonnaded structure, it was entered and exited by ramps at the front and back, and contained only a resting-place where the divine barque was placed during rituals. The exterior is covered with fine reliefs of Senusret I making offerings to the gods and goddesses on behalf of his people.

Senusret I's policies were continued by his successors Amenemhat II and Senusret II, and by the time of Senusret III (*c*.1874–*c*.1855BCE), Egypt's former power had been reestablished in Nubia and Syria-Palestine. Egypt's southern boundary was pushed south to the second Nile Cataract at Semna, and the completion of a chain

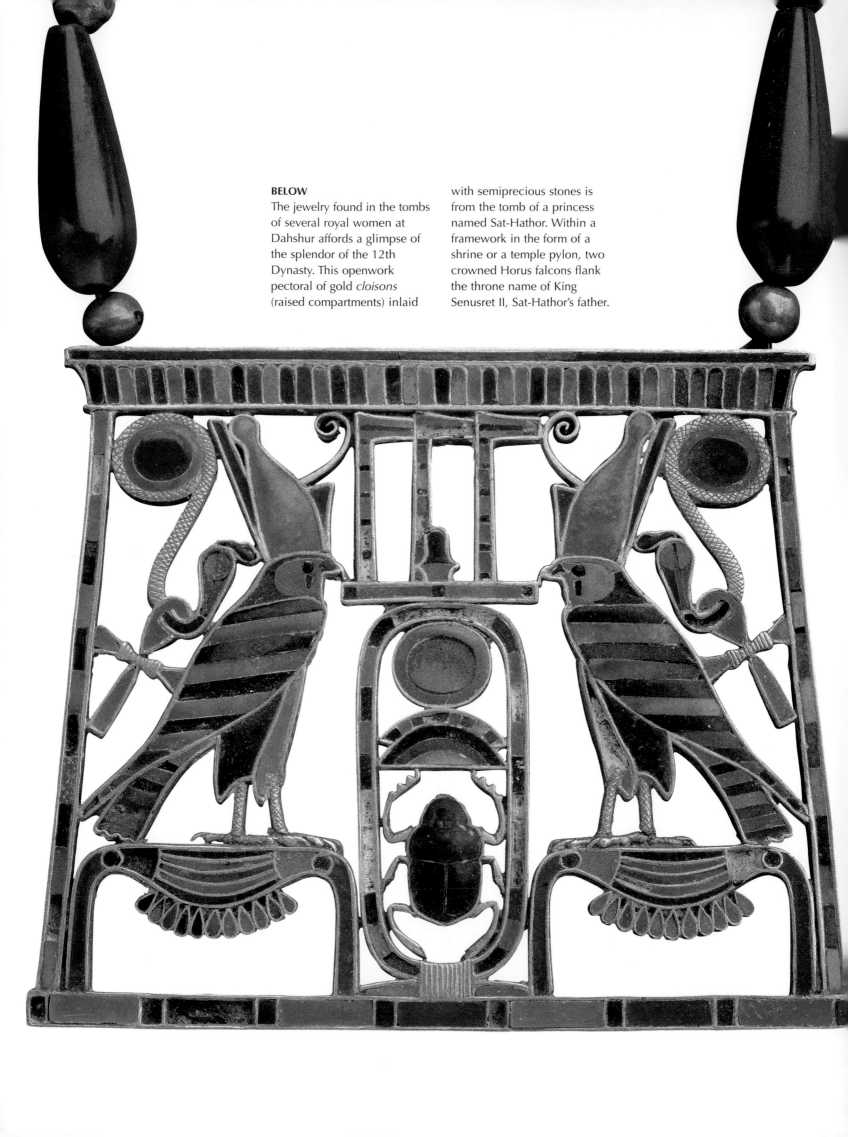

**BELOW**

The jewelry found in the tombs of several royal women at Dahshur affords a glimpse of the splendor of the 12th Dynasty. This openwork pectoral of gold *cloisons* (raised compartments) inlaid with semiprecious stones is from the tomb of a princess named Sat-Hathor. Within a framework in the form of a shrine or a temple pylon, two crowned Horus falcons flank the throne name of King Senusret II, Sat-Hathor's father.

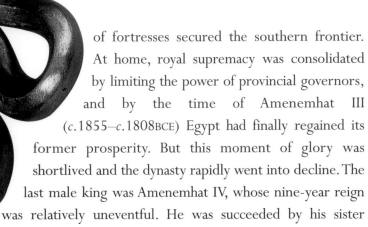

of fortresses secured the southern frontier. At home, royal supremacy was consolidated by limiting the power of provincial governors, and by the time of Amenemhat III (*c*.1855–*c*.1808BCE) Egypt had finally regained its former prosperity. But this moment of glory was shortlived and the dynasty rapidly went into decline. The last male king was Amenemhat IV, whose nine-year reign was relatively uneventful. He was succeeded by his sister Sobekneferu, the first woman known with absolute certainty to have ruled as pharaoh. In her brief reign (*c*.1799–*c*.1795BCE), the last of the dynasty, she is believed to have completed the vast mortuary temple of Amenemhat III at Hawara near Lahun in the north, which was said to contain 3,000 chambers and was later called "the Labyrinth" by the Greeks after their myth of the Minotaur.

Sobeknefru's own burial place is not known for certain but, like the tombs of all the kings of the 12th Dynasty, it was probably in the north at a site such as Lisht, Lahun, or Dahshur. Here, the dynasty revived the Old Kingdom pyramid-building tradition. Members of the royal family and high officials were also buried in these cemeteries; some tombs of royal women have yielded magnificent examples of jewelry.

As a result, there are few remarkable funerary monuments of this date to be found in Thebes; instead, kings and other high-status individuals recorded their presence at Thebes by dedicating statues of themselves in Theban temples. The only known 12th-Dynasty decorated tomb at Thebes was originally intended for a high official named Inyotef-iqer, the vizier of Senusret I, but it was used instead for the burial of his mother Senet—Inyotef-iqer himself was buried at Lisht. Far more common are the undecorated tombs of lesser Theban officials, such as the steward Montuhotep, whose modest burial was uncovered intact in 1823.

**LEFT**
The regalia of King Senusret II (*c*.1847–*c*.1837BCE) included this cobra of gold and semiprecious stones, which would have been worn on the front of the king's crown or headdress, symbolically rearing up to spit poison into the eyes of the king's enemies. Known by the Greek term *uraeus* (which may mean "she who rears up"), the cobra was often identified with the cobra-goddess Wadjyt, the patron deity of Lower Egypt, whose cult dated to predynastic times.

**RIGHT**

A painted limestone stela from the tomb of Nit-Ptah, a royal official of the 12th Dynasty, and his family, excavated in the Asasif area of western Thebes by the New York Metropolitan Museum of Art in 1915. Just 9 inches (23 cm) high by 1 foot (31 cm) wide, the stela shows Nit-Ptah and his wife Seni (center) flanked by their daughter Dedu and their son Inyotef (Antef). The act of smelling a lotus or water lily alludes to the rejuvenation of the body after death. The inscription across the top of the stela records that the tomb owner and his family, in the presence of the funerary deity Ptah-Sokar, have acquired the status of *imakhu* ("honored person" or "admired person").

# RIVALS FOR THE KINGDOM
## THE 13TH TO 17TH DYNASTIES (C.1795–C.1550BCE)

The 12th Dynasty kings were succeeded by another Theban family, the 13th Dynasty (*c*.1795BCE–*c*.1650BCE), who initially continued to rule Egypt from the north. However, there was little continuity of rule, with over 60 kings in 150 years, and this political weakness led to challenges by rivals including the 14th Dynasty, who ruled parts of Egypt at the same time as the 13th Dynasty.

Distracted by internal issues, the Thebans found themselves unable to assert control over Egypt's borders. Nubia slipped from Egyptian domination, while the Nile Delta saw large influxes of Asiatic peoples from Syria and Palestine, who eventually established an independent kingdom governed from the city of Avaris. These rulers (the 15th and 16th Dynasties) were known to the Egyptians as the *heka khaswt* ("foreign rulers"), a term that the Greeks later rendered as "Hyksos."

Later Egyptian texts suggest that the Hyksos occupation was an aggressive invasion by a foreign power, but in reality it was probably a gradual immigration, and relations between the Thebans and the Hyksos seem at first to have been friendly. The Hyksos were essentially herders and traders and showed little interest in expanding southward into the Nile Valley. In time, however, the relationship began to sour as the Hyksos consolidated their power in the Delta and the Thebans were excluded from Near Eastern trade. Finding their sphere of influence increasingly confined to the southern Nile Valley, the 13th Dynasty moved their capital back to Thebes.

The city has not yielded a great deal of archaeological evidence of the embattled 13th Dynasty, but more survives from the time of their eventual successors, the 17th Dynasty (*c*.1650–*c*.1550BCE). These kings and their queens were buried in the Dra Abu el-Naga area of the Theban west bank, although the precise location of the tombs, excavated in the 19th century, has been lost. Royal burial

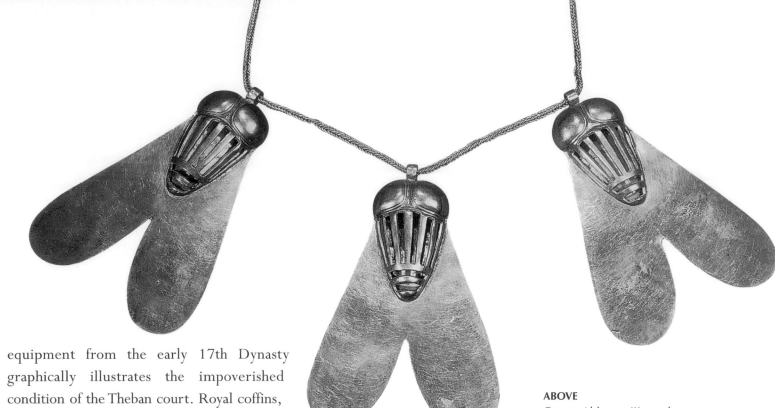

equipment from the early 17th Dynasty graphically illustrates the impoverished condition of the Theban court. Royal coffins, traditionally constructed of cedar from Lebanon and richly ornamented with Nubian gold, were now made from local wood and covered with thin gold leaf. Known as *rishi* (the Arabic for "feather"), these coffins were of a new design, representing the king folded in the feathered wings of protective goddesses.

It was not until the reign of Seqenenra Taa II, late in the 17th Dynasty (*c.*1560BCE), that the Thebans began actively to oppose the Hyksos kings of the north. This increased hostility is reflected in a later text called *The Quarrel of Apepi and Seqenenra* that has the Hyksos king Apepi writing to Seqenenra from Avaris to complain that the hippopotami of Thebes are keeping him awake with their roaring. However, a more sober and concrete witness to the conflict is the battle-scarred mummy of Seqenenra. A scientific examination of the gashes in his skull suggests that some of them were inflicted by an ax of Palestinian design—supporting the idea that the king died fighting the Hyksos.

Seqenenra was succeeded by his son Kamose (*c.*1555–*c.*1550BCE), whose victories over the Hyksos and their Nubian allies are recorded on two stelae erected in the temple of Amun at Karnak. Kamose's reign was short, but by the end of it the Thebans had captured Avaris and driven the Hyksos back into southern Palestine. Since Kamose's successor, his brother Ahmose I, was still a child, the government of Egypt fell to their mother, Queen Ahhotep I, the widow of Seqenenra. In later times, Ahhotep's key role at this critical period of Egypt's history was acknowledged in monuments and inscriptions describing her achievements. Her coffin was found among the royal mummies removed for safekeeping to a single tomb at Deir el-Bahri (DB320) in the 22nd Dynasty.

**ABOVE**
Queen Ahhotep II's tomb also yielded a ceremonial golden dagger and ax of Ahmose I (see page 47), and this magnificent necklace with pendants of three golden flies—a regal version of the "flies of valor" awarded to victorious soldiers. These relatively unusual pieces were perhaps given to her in acknowledgment of her role during the wars of reunification.

# EXPLORATION AND DISCOVERY

**ABOVE**
A painting from the tomb of Sety I (KV17) copied by Giovanni Battista Belzoni, who found the tomb in 1817. Belzoni was not primarily an artist but his copies remain a valuable record of the tomb's paintings and inscriptions, which have deteriorated considerably since his time.

Throughout antiquity the city of Thebes was a powerful attraction to travelers and scholars, as attested by the profusion of Greek and Latin graffiti found on Theban monuments. Until modern times, the accounts of Classical writers, such as the Greek historians Herodotus and Diodorus and the geographer Strabo, were the principal sources of information on ancient Egypt available to Western readers.

In the Middle Ages, Western pilgrims to the Holy Land continued to visit the pyramids and other Lower Egyptian sites, but the distant south of Egypt lapsed into obscurity. The earliest recorded visits to Thebes by Westerners after Roman times date from the late 17th and early 18th centuries. In 1715, a French Jesuit priest, Claude Sicard, became the first European scholar since antiquity to identify the site of the ancient city; using Classical sources he also identified such monuments as the Colossi of Memnon and the Valley of the Kings. His discoveries paved the way for later explorers such as the Dane Frederik Ludwig Norden and the Briton Richard Pococke, who visited Thebes separately in 1737–8 and were the first to make plans and sketches of some of the royal tombs. Local hostility toward strangers made the work of these early researchers difficult and dangerous.

The first large-scale exploration of Thebes began in 1798, when Napoleon occupied Egypt (then a province of the Ottoman Empire) as part of a bid to control trade routes to India. His army brought a party of engineers, draughtsmen, and scholars whose mission included a detailed survey of all Egypt's monuments. Their discoveries included the Rosetta Stone, which was to provide the key to the decipherment of the hieroglyphic script. The British expelled the French army in 1801, but the scholars were allowed to remain, and the result was the monumental *Description de L'Egypte* (24 volumes, 1809–22), which stimulated a huge interest in Egyptian antiquities.

In 1816 Giovanni Battista Belzoni was commissioned to transport part of a fallen statue of "the Younger Memnon"—Ramesses II—to England from the king's mortuary temple in Thebes. In this contemporary view Belzoni's Egyptian workforce haul the colossal fragment, which weighs more than 7 tons (7,000 kg) and is 9 feet (2.7 m) high, to the Nile River prior to its shipment to London. It now resides in the British Museum.

The interior of what the early scholars of Egypt referred to as the "Memnonium" and "the tomb of Ozymandias"—the mortuary temple of Ramesses II in western Thebes, known today as the Ramesseum. The hand-tinted engraving comes from the great *Description de l'Egypte* (1809–22), which sparked a huge interest in ancient Egypt. Owing to the accuracy of its illustrations the work remains a useful resource for Egyptologists.

**ABOVE**

*The Battle at the Temple of Karnak* (oil on canvas) by Jean-Charles Langlois (1789–1870), a French army officer-turned-painter celebrated for his dramatic panoramas. The work depicts a French victory over the Turks in 1799 during Napoleon's expedition to Egypt, but the painting is dominated by the imposing and atmospheric ruins of Karnak, viewed looking west toward the 1st Pylon. The temple of Luxor is visible in the distance (top left).

The monuments of Thebes were made more accessible by Muhammad Ali (1805–49), the reforming Ottoman viceroy of Egypt, and became a magnet for scholars and collectors. Many of the most active collectors were diplomats, such as the French consul-general Bernardino Drovetti and his British counterpart Henry Salt, who acquired large collections of Theban antiquities respectively for the Musée du Louvre in Paris and the British Museum in London. Salt's agent, the Italian engineer and former circus strongman Giovanni Belzoni, was responsible for the discovery and excavation of many important monuments, including the tomb of Sety I in the Valley of the Kings.

The decipherment of the hieroglyphs by the French scholar Jean-François Champollion in 1822 initiated a more scholarly approach to the study of Egyptian antiquities, with greater emphasis on recording and describing monuments and artifacts. In 1828 Champollion and Ippolito Rosellini led a Franco-Italian expedition to Egypt and spent two and a half months at Thebes; in 1844–5 a German expedition under

Carl Richard Lepsius spent a season recording and collecting Theban antiquities. Among the many British scholars who pioneered the scientific study of the Theban monuments were Robert Hay, James Burton, Alexander Rhind, and John Gardner Wilkinson. Wilkinson remained at Thebes from 1821 to 1832, living in a house he had built around a tomb at Qurna. During this time he made meticulous copies of thousands of inscriptions and tomb paintings, many of which have since deteriorated badly or been lost altogether, making his work a uniquely valuable record.

For decades excavations at Thebes were largely unregulated, and looting and vandalism were rife. In 1858 Muhammad Ali's son and successor, Said Pasha, appointed the French scholar Auguste Mariette as Egypt's first Director of Antiquities, and the Egyptian Antiquities Service was created. Mariette's discoveries at Thebes included the tombs of the 17th Dynasty kings at Dra Abu el-Naga, since lost.

The aim of the Antiquities Service was twofold: to regulate archaeological work in Egypt; and to record and preserve its monuments and artifacts. By the end of the century, the Theban monuments were under the supervision of an Inspector of Antiquities appointed by the Service, and the indiscriminate export of antiquities had been banned. A system of concessions for archaeological work had been implemented, and although private individuals continued to fund excavations, systematic exploration was increasingly under the auspices of learned institutions such as universities and museums.

A series of spectacular discoveries around the turn of the 20th century brought Thebes to the attention of the world and stimulated a wave of public

**BELOW**
The entrance to Luxor temple, a lithograph by the Scottish artist David Roberts (1796–1864). It comes from *Egypt and Nubia*, a stunning visual record of Roberts' travels in Egypt and the Near East in 1838–9. It shows the temple before centuries of debris had been cleared—but not before one of the two obelisks had been removed to Paris.

**ABOVE**
Howard Carter opens the doors
of the nested shrines enclosing
the sarcophagus, three coffins,
and mummy of Tutankhamun.
Carter's associate, Arthur
Callender, and an unnamed
Egyptian workman look on.

**OPPOSITE**
Carter brushes away fragments
of a linen shroud from the
second coffin of Tutankhamun,
prior to its removal. Carter
completed his painstaking
clearance and conservation
of the contents of KV62 only
in 1932, ten years after the
tomb's discovery.

interest in Egyptology. In 1881 Mariette's successor, Gaston Maspero, excavated a cache of 40 royal mummies that had been reburied in antiquity after their tombs had been robbed. In 1898 Victor Loret discovered another group of royal mummies in the tomb of Amenhotep II. Excavations at Karnak in 1903 yielded more than 8,000 objects, including more than 1,000 stone sculptures buried during temple remodeling in ancient times.

The most famous discovery at Thebes was Howard Carter's location in 1922 of the tomb of Tutankhamun, with its unimagined treasures (see pages 98–119). The impact of this spectacular discovery has tended to overshadow the equally important but less glamorous work of Ernesto Schiaparelli (1905–9) and Bernard Bruyère (1917–47) at Deir el-Medina, and the painstaking recording of private tombs by New York's Metropolitan Museum of Art (1907–38). Often overlooked, too, are the efforts of the Antiquities Service to secure and conserve the monuments. Arthur Weigall, an Inspector of Antiquities at Thebes in the early 1900s, initiated much of this work, and also introduced the modern tomb-numbering system.

Excavations at Thebes continue, with each season bringing new discoveries, most notably in recent years the tomb of the many sons of Ramesses II (KV5). But even greater emphasis is now given to conservation. The enormous number of visitors, air pollution, and a rise in the water table caused by the construction of the Aswan High Dam have led to a dramatic deterioration in the fabric of the Theban monuments, making recording and preservation work more pressing than ever. New research methods, archaeological techniques, and conservation technologies are constantly in development to ensure that the heritage of Thebes can be studied and enjoyed by future generations.

**AHMOSE I**
1550–1525BCE

**AMENHOTEP I**
1525–1504BCE

**THUTMOSE I**
1504–1492BCE

**THUTMOSE II**
1492–1479BCE

**HATSHEPSUT**
1479–1458BCE

**THUTMOSE III**
1479–1425BCE

**AMENHOTEP I**
1427–1400BCE

**HUTMOSE IV**
**1400–1390BCE**

**AMENHOTEP III**
**1390–1352BCE**

**AMENHOTEP IV**
**(AKHENATEN)**
**1352–1336BCE**

**TUTANKHAMUN**
**1336–1327BCE**

**AY**
**1327–1323BCE**

**HOREMHEB**
**1323–1295BCE**

# MOST FAVORED OF PLACES

### THE 18TH DYNASTY (C.1550–C.1295BCE)

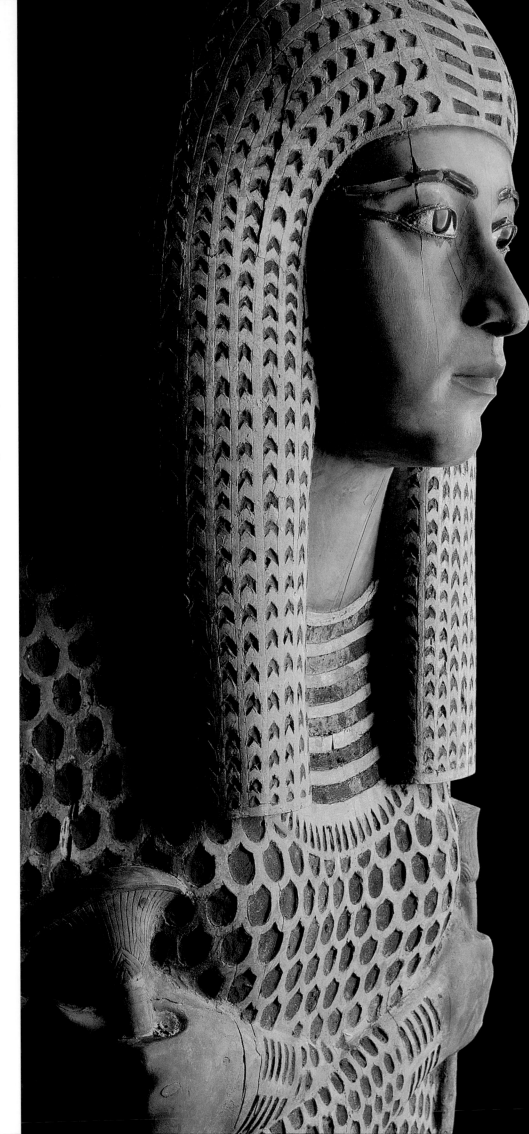

**RIGHT**
The beautiful cedarwood coffin of Queen Ahmose Meritamun, daughter of Ahmose I and Queen Ahmose Nefertari, and sister and wife of King Amenhotep I, from her tomb (DB358) at Deir el-Bahri in western Thebes. A nearby temple, later removed to make way for the mortuary temple of Hatshepsut, may have served as the mortuary temple for both Meritamun's mother and her husband, where they were worshiped after death.

**OPPOSITE**
A ceremonial axhead inscribed with the name of King Ahmose I, who is shown smiting an Asiatic captive above an image of a griffin and the inscription "Beloved of [the war god] Montu." Ahmose's expulsion of the Hyksos, the Asiatic rulers of the Delta, and his consolidation of Egypt's reunification earned him the status of a dynastic founder in Egyptian eyes.

# UNITY RESTORED

## AHMOSE I AND AMENHOTEP I (C.1550–C.1504BCE)

With the expulsion of the Hyksos, Egypt was once more a united kingdom. Although there was no change in the ruling family, Ahmose I (*c*.1550–*c*.1525BCE) is regarded as the first pharaoh of the 18th Dynasty. Under this dynasty Egypt reached the peak of its international power and prestige, and it was also the "golden age" of the city of Thebes.

Much of Ahmose I's adult career was spent on campaign in Nubia and Syria-Palestine, reasserting Egyptian power in these regions and laying the foundations of Egypt's future empire. At home, Queen Ahmose Nefertari oversaw her husband's reconstruction programs, helping to reorganize the national administration and to rebuild long-neglected religious monuments. After Ahmose's death, she held the reins of power while their son, Amenhotep I (*c*.1525–*c*.1504BCE), grew to adulthood.

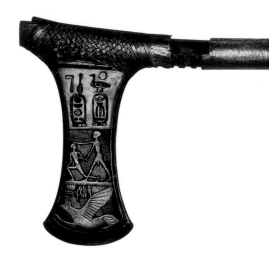

Just as Kamose had dedicated his victories to Amun by erecting stelae at Karnak, Ahmose and Amenhotep I took care to beautify the temples of Thebes. Among their surviving monuments are a finely carved lintel of Ahmose, now in the British Museum, and an exquisite alabaster barque shrine of Amenhotep I at Karnak.

The early 18th Dynasty also marked a change in royal burial practices. Earlier royal tombs had been based on the *saff* model, combining one or more burial chambers with a chapel where offerings were made to the dead king. However, it seems that from the time of Amenhotep I kings were buried in tombs cut into the solid rock of a remote wadi on the Theban west bank—the Valley of the Kings. Unlike their precursors, these tombs had concealed entrances and no integral offering chapels; instead, the cult of the dead monarch was celebrated in a separate mortuary temple elsewhere in the Theban necropolis. Amenhotep I's tomb has not been conclusively identified, but it was probably the one known today as KV39 (that is, Tomb 39 in the Valley of the Kings).

Amenhotep I and Ahmose Nefertari were also recognized as the founders of the tomb builders' village at Deir el-Medina (see pages 156–63). In time, the deified king and his mother became the village's patron deities, worshiped in both public and private shrines and celebrated at an annual festival.

# A VALLEY FOR THE KINGS
## THUTMOSE I AND THUTMOSE II (c.1504–c.1479 BCE)

Amenhotep I was succeeded by his son Thutmose I (*c.*1504–*c.*1492 BCE) and grandson Thutmose II (*c.*1492–*c.*1479 BCE), who continued to expand and consolidate the Egyptian empire. Between them, these two Theban kings extended Egyptian rule in Nubia as far as the third Nile cataract, and established control over a large area of the Levant. Once more, Egypt prospered from African and Near Eastern commerce, as mining and trading expeditions were resumed.

Although the political capital had probably returned to Memphis by this time, Thebes reaped its share of the country's new wealth. Under Thutmose I, the temple of Amun at Karnak was enclosed by a massive stone wall with an impressive pylon (gateway). Inside, a second new pylon led into the temple sanctuary. In front of the new entrance, a pair of magnificent granite obelisks proclaimed the king's glory. Nearby, a new treasury was constructed to store the valuable royal gifts flowing into the temple coffers. Thutmose II added a festival court and a second pair of obelisks in front of the temple entrance.

On the west bank, lavish new royal tombs and temples testified to the new era of prosperity. Thutmose I was the first king known for certain to have been buried in the Valley of the Kings: his architect, Ineni, was later to boast how he had constructed the tomb in secret, "nobody seeing, nobody hearing." In fact the king seems to have had two tombs. The first, KV20 (probably the one Ineni refers to), was enlarged by his daughter Hatshepsut, who probably intended to share it with her father; but her successor, Thutmose III, seems to have reburied his grandfather in another tomb, KV38. Thutmose I's original tomb comprised a series of corridors and stairways terminating in a burial chamber decorated with funerary drawings and inscriptions.

The tomb of Thutmose II has yet to be identified, but was probably of a similar design. He built a mortuary temple close to that of his father, and his mummy was discovered reburied in the Deir el-Bahri cache. Other members of the royal family were buried in tombs in valleys adjacent to the Valley of the Kings.

**OPPOSITE**
A granite obelisk (right) erected by Thutmose I at Karnak, one of four that once stood before the 4th Pylon, which he built as a new ceremonial entrance to the temple. Obelisks were popular in the New Kingdom, when most of these tall monuments to the sun were erected. Weighing in the region of 140 tons (143,000 kg), this monolith stands 72 feet (22 m) high and bears three columns of inscription on each face, the central column being a dedication by the king. Its tip would once have been gilded to catch the rays of the rising sun. The obelisk to the left was erected a few decades later by Thutmose I's daughter, Hatshepsut (see pages 50–53).

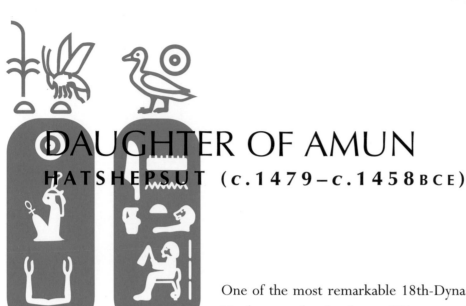

# DAUGHTER OF AMUN
## HATSHEPSUT (c.1479–c.1458bce)

One of the most remarkable 18th-Dynasty rulers to leave their mark on Thebes was Hatshepsut, the daughter of Thutmose I and principal queen of Thutmose II. When Thutmose II died, early in his reign, Hatshepsut had not produced a male heir, so the throne passed to his son by a minor wife. But since the new king, the future Thutmose III, was still a child, it was natural for his father's senior queen to act as regent for the young pharaoh, much as other queens had done before her. Initially Hatshepsut conformed to this role, but later assumed the throne as pharaoh in her own right.

Hatshepsut's action was a radical departure from royal tradition, which demanded a man on the throne—the king was, above all, the living embodiment of the male god Horus. In order to govern Egypt, therefore, Hatshepsut had to present her court and subjects with a convincing male image. She adopted the titles of a king and—at least in public art—appeared in male royal costume, wearing the traditional false beard of a pharaoh. To validate her unconventional position, Hatshepsut propagated the myth that she was not in fact mortal, but the divine child of the god Amun, to whom she always referred as her "divine father." The support of the increasingly powerful priests of Amun at Thebes was crucial, and much of her reign was devoted to building monuments to the god, especially at Karnak and Deir el-Bahri.

The choice of these significant sites, indelibly associated with the earliest Theban kings, was undoubtedly influenced by one of Hatshepsut's important allies, her architect and adviser Senenmut. Few architects' names survive from ancient Egypt, and fewer still appear to have enjoyed the intimacy that Senenmut shared with the royal family. His elder brother had been tutor to Hatshepsut when she was a girl, and Senenmut in turn became tutor to her daughter Neferura. His name appears alongside that of Hatshepsut on several monuments and he was granted the extraordinary privilege of building his own tomb within the precincts of her mortuary temple at Deir el-Bahri.

At Karnak, Hatshepsut's monuments included an elegant chapel of red quartzite and a pair of gilded granite obelisks, the northernmost of which remains

**OPPOSITE**
A monumental head of Hatshepsut, part of a painted statue that stood in her mortuary temple at Deir el-Bahri. She is represented as the god Osiris, lord of the dead, with whom all kings were identified after death, and wears the long false beard of a male deity.

where it was raised in front of her father's pylon. Obelisks were a favorite vehicle for royal propaganda, since they were comparatively quick to erect, yet occupied little space. Above all, they were highly visible. The tips of Hatshepsut's obelisks were gilded to catch the rays of the rising sun, proclaiming her glory and magnificence throughout the surrounding countryside. The sides were carved with reliefs and texts confirming Hatshepsut's legitimacy and her special relationship to the gods, such as this inscription from the base of her northern obelisk (see page 49): "She made her monuments for her father Amun, lord of the thrones of the Two Lands, in front of Karnak, making for him two great obelisks of hard granite from the south, the sides covered with the finest gold in the land so that they could be seen from both sides of the river, flooding the Two Lands with their rays when the *aten* [sun disc] shines between as it rises in the horizon of the sky."

A little way south of Karnak, Hatshepsut erected a shrine for the Opet festival—an annual fertility rite (see page 80)—on what was later to be the site of Amenhotep III's great temple of Luxor. Long-established religious centers such as the Karnak complex offered only limited opportunities for architectural expression among the crowded monuments of former kings. Existing buildings were often demolished by subsequent rulers to make way for new ones: thus Hatshepsut's red quartzite chapel at Karnak was later dismantled and its blocks reused as filling for a new pylon.

In contrast, the mortuary temples on the west bank at Thebes were by definition always new foundations, and ones which rulers and their architects could use as powerful propaganda statements. The temple erected by Hatshepsut for the veneration of her deified self after death was named the "Sublime of Sublimes" and was dedicated to herself and her father, Thutmose I. Its site, set against the sheer cliff face of Deir el-Bahri alongside Mentuhotep II's earlier tomb and temple, was a political statement in itself, and one that was reinforced by its superior scale—it is more than twice the size of her predecessor's monument.

**OPPOSITE, ABOVE**
The head of the goddess Hathor adorns a pillar of the middle terrace of Hatshepsut's mortuary temple at Deir el-Bahri in western Thebes. As the "Lady of the West," Hathor nightly greeted the sun god as he descended into the underworld, where she protected him until the dawn. At Thebes the funerary monuments of royalty and ordinary citizens alike ask the goddess to provide the deceased similar protection.

**OPPOSITE, BELOW**
With its monumental ramps and terraces and dramatic backdrop of cliffs and crags, Hatshepsut's extraordinary mortuary temple clearly echoes the design of the tomb and temple of her illustrious 11th-Dynasty predecessor, Mentuhotep II. The remains of Mentuhotep's far smaller monument can be seen in the background, alongside Hatshepsut's temple.

The design, with its dramatic terraces joined by sloping ramps, was clearly influenced by the earlier building. Like Mentuhotep's monument, Hatshepsut's complex originally included a "valley temple" connected to the main temple by a causeway lined with sphinxes, and was surrounded by gardens with ponds and avenues of trees. The terraced design of the temple provided large areas for relief carving, although—unlike other New Kingdom pharaohs, whose monuments are covered with scenes of battles and foreign conquest—Hatshepsut seems to have preferred to record her more peaceful achievements for posterity.

The best-preserved reliefs are found in the southern colonnade of the middle terrace. These commemorate a two-year trading expedition to the incense-producing African land of Punt (probably somewhere in the region of modern Somalia), narrating the story in cartoon-strip fashion. On the northern side of the terrace, a very damaged series of scenes justifies Hatshepsut's claim to the throne by illustrating her conception and birth as a legitimate child of Amun.

Hatshepsut ruled Egypt successfully for 15 years, and her reign was apparently one of peace and prosperity. However, her eventual fate remains a mystery: after Thutmose III's accession as sole ruler she simply disappears from the record, and it is not known how the transition of power occurred. On Thutmose III's orders, Hatshepsut's name was removed from public monuments and records, but the fact that this was not carried out until late in his reign suggests that it was more an act of propriety—a female king was simply not ideologically acceptable—than of revenge. Her body has so far not been identified: both her original tomb, cut high in the cliffs of a remote Theban valley northeast of the Valley of the Queens, and the burial chamber that she prepared in her father's tomb in the Valley of the Kings (KV20) were found empty. It is possible that she may have been buried elsewhere, perhaps by Thutmose III; it has been suggested that a female mummy found in another tomb in the Valley of the Kings (KV60) may be Hatshepsut.

# YEARS OF CONQUEST
## THUTMOSE III (C.1479–C.1425 BCE)

The son of Thutmose II and Aset (Isis), a minor royal wife, Thutmose III enjoyed one of the longest reigns—54 years—of any pharaoh. However, his first 20 years as king were spent in the shadow of his stepmother, Hatshepsut, and it was only from *c*.1458BCE that he fully held the reins of power. Thutmose III enjoys a reputation as one of Egypt's great warrior kings. In his first year of sole kingship he consolidated Egyptian power in the Syria-Palestine region by defeating the forces of Qadesh and Mittani, and subsequently maintained order throughout his domains through energetic military and diplomatic action. By the end of his reign, the Egyptian empire stretched from the 4th Nile Cataract in the south to the borders of modern Turkey in the north.

At home, Thutmose was careful to cultivate the support of the Theban priesthood of Amun by erecting new temple buildings and enriching the god's temples with the spoils of war. He also completed many of Hatshepsut's monuments at Karnak and Luxor on the east bank of the Nile, and at Medinet Habu on the west bank. It is likely that his aim in doing this was twofold: to establish his own monuments while obscuring his predecessor's propaganda.

At Karnak, Thutmose III completed Hatshepsut's pylon (today referred to as the 8th Pylon), built to mark the beginning of a planned new processional route linking Karnak and Luxor. He also raised his own pylon (the 7th Pylon—the modern numbering is not chronological), between Hatshepsut's pylon and the main temple axis. Much of Thutmose's redevelopment work at Karnak concentrated on the sanctuary area, where Hatshepsut had begun an extensive renewal plan. He remodeled a pair of chapels built by Hatshepsut and walled in her obelisks, added more shrines and enclosed the sanctuary with a wall recording his foreign campaigns. Between the sanctuary and the 5th Pylon of his grandfather Thutmose I, he erected yet another gateway (the 6th Pylon).

Behind the sanctuary area, a special hall was constructed for the celebration of Thutmose's Jubilee festival. Known as the Heb-Sed, this ancient royal

**OPPOSITE**
A fine, half-lifesize green graywacke statue of Thutmose III from Karnak, a temple much embellished by the king during his lengthy reign. He is portrayed wearing a kilt and the royal striped *nemes* headcloth, which had two lappets or flaps over the shoulders and was gathered into a pigtail at the back. On his brow the *uraeus* cobra rears up, symbolically defending him from his enemies (see also illustration on page 33).

**OPPOSITE**
Paintings from the tomb chapel
of Rekhmira at Sheikh Abd
el-Qurna. Rekhmira was vizier
of Upper Egypt, governor of
Thebes, and steward of the
temple of Amun under kings
Thutmose III and Amenhotep
II, and befitting his eminent
status his tomb is one of the
most remarkable in western
Thebes. Among its many
unique scenes are depictions
of its owner's life and duties,
which included overseeing the
artisans of Karnak, among
them metalworkers (seen here
smelting bronze over a fire),
brickmakers, carpenters, and
many others.

rite was usually held in or around the 25th year of a king's reign. During the festival, the king reasserted his competence to rule by completing a series of strenuous rituals that included lassoing a wild bull and running around a course symbolizing Egypt's boundaries. Following these ceremonies, the king underwent a second coronation ritual to confirm his status.

Thutmose's festival hall recalls the ancient origins of the Jubilee in its unusual columns, which are shaped like the tent poles that supported the traditional temporary shrines used for the ceremonies. Its decoration notably included a scene of Thutmose III worshiping the names of previous kings (see page 19), emphasizing his determination to be identified as the rightful successor to the throne of Egypt.

As a result of Thutmose's military campaigns, Egypt experienced unprecedented wealth, together with a large influx of foreign captives and migrants. Among their ranks were many specialized craftsmen such as weavers, embroiderers, metalworkers, and perhaps glassmakers too—the first datable piece of Egyptian glass was made at this time. These artisans contributed to an opulent and cosmopolitan atmosphere that also extended to the royal court. Thutmose III is known to have had several foreign wives, and the tomb of three minor queens of Syrian descent contained vast quantities of spectacular jewelry, cosmetics, and perfume.

Private tombs of Thutmose's reign provide further insights into life in Thebes at this time. The vizier Rekhmira, who served under Thutmose III and his son Amenhotep II, was the highest official in the land, a position reflected in his magnificent tomb (TT100) at Sheikh Abd el-Qurna on the west bank. It is a typical New Kingdom rock-cut tomb, with an external courtyard and an offering chapel shaped like an upturned letter T. The chapel is decorated with finely painted and colorful scenes of Rekhmira's life, official duties, and funeral, and records the arrival of exotic commodities from the farthest corners of the empire, a court of justice in session, and the factories, stores, and workshops at Karnak.

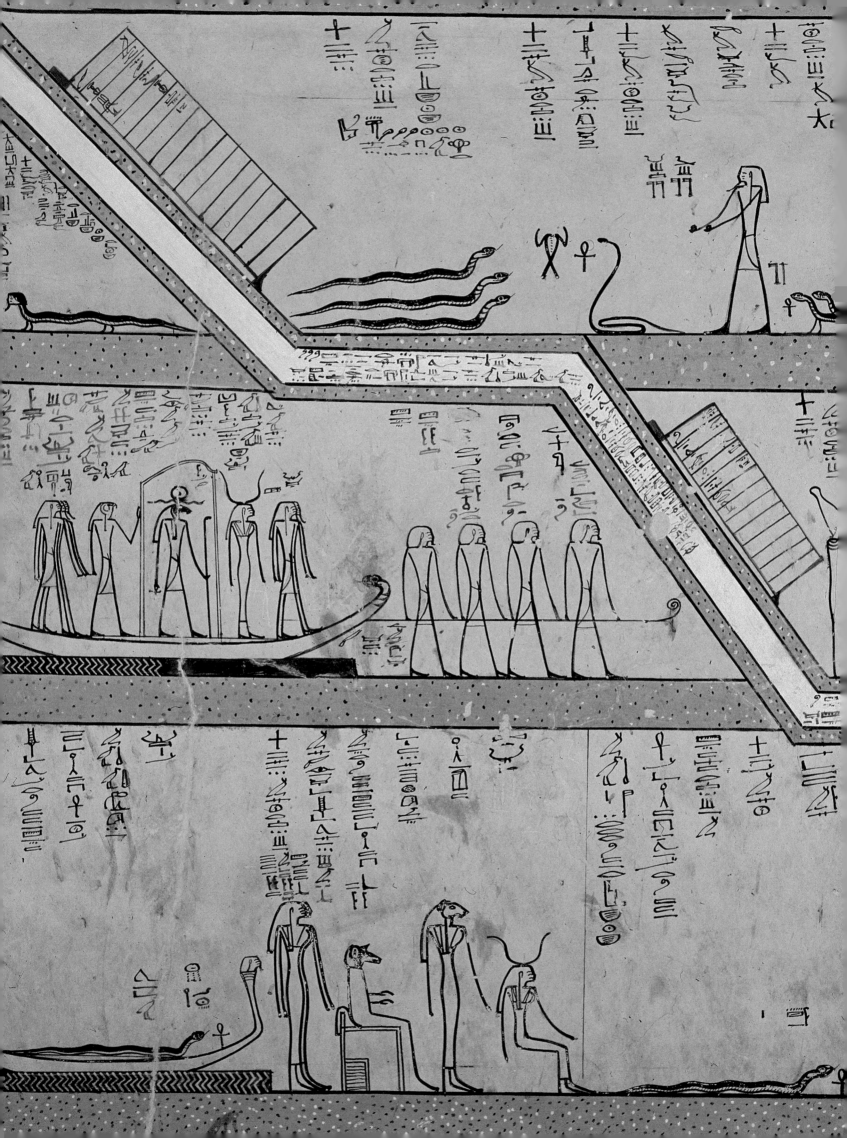

The tomb of Thutmose III himself (KV34) is one of the most impressive in the Valley of the Kings, both in terms of its dramatic location and its groundbreaking design and decoration. Situated high in the cliffs at the southernmost end of the valley, its entrance passage plunges steeply downward, ending abruptly at a deep, rectangular well sunk into the floor

The purpose of this enigmatic feature—the first in the Valley of the Kings—has been the subject of much discussion. One argument is that the well was intended as a trap to foil tomb robbers; another is that it was meant to protect the royal burial by preventing rainwater from flowing into the lower chambers. Another possibility is that it served some ritual or symbolic purpose. Beyond the well, a large rectangular antechamber is decorated with paintings of underworld deities. The entrance to the burial chamber, which is oriented at a right angle to the main axis, was via a concealed staircase in a corner of the floor.

The vast oval burial chamber has four side rooms intended to contain the royal grave goods. At the far end is Thutmose's granite sarcophagus: shaped like a royal cartouche, it is carved with images of protective goddesses. The paintings on the walls imitate the cursive script and graphic style of a funerary papyrus, executed in muted tones of black on cream, with pink and red highlights. The scenes are taken from the funerary text known as *Amduat* ("*The Book of What is in the Underworld*"), and narrate the sun god's nightly descent into the underworld and his passage through the twelve hours of the night. In this metaphor for his own death and rebirth, the king aids the gods in defeating Apep, the serpent of chaos, thus ensuring both the sun's daily rebirth and his own resurrection.

Little else survives from the tomb, which was thoroughly pillaged in antiquity. However, the rifled and rewrapped body of Thutmose III was among the cache of royal mummies found at Deir el-Bahri (DB320), inside one of its original wooden coffins from which every trace of inlay and gilding had been hacked off.

# KARNAK AND THE CULT OF AMUN

OPPOSITE AND BELOW
The 134 massive columns of Karnak's Great Hypostyle Hall, were erected by Sety I and their carvings completed by his son Ramesses II; they cover an area of some 64,500 sq feet (6,000 sq m). Reliefs on the walls include the scene below, which shows the kneeling figure of Ramesses II with the Theban divine triad of Amun-Ra, Egypt's supreme national deity, his consort Mut, and, behind Amun-Ra's throne, their son Khonsu.

By the New Kingdom, the "Estate of Amun" at Thebes had become one of the most important and powerful institutions in Egypt. The Theban god Amun, the "Hidden One," had been fused with Ra, the sun god of Heliopolis in northern Egypt, to create a supreme deity—Amun-Ra—and Thebes became known as the "Southern Heliopolis."

Since the king was the sole intermediary between humanity and the gods, he was in theory the high priest of every temple, and is the only figure shown making offerings to the deities in temple sanctuaries. In practice, however, his everyday religious duties were delegated to the priests of each temple. The priestly hierarchy descended from the high priest, or First Prophet, who acted as the king's proxy, to the humble attendants responsible for cleaning and other menial work.

The aim of Egyptian religion was the maintenance of divine order in both the state and the cosmos, and so the concepts of religious service and social order were inseparable. Although the temple, or "God's House," was primarily a religious institution, it also served as a local administrative center, incorporating government offices, schools, and law courts. The temple workshops not only supplied the needs of the priesthood, but also produced divine images, amulets, tomb equipment, and funerary papyri for private individuals. Taxation revenues were held in temple stores and granaries to be redistributed as wages to state employees, and many of the temple staff were civil servants whose posts required them to carry out part-time priestly duties.

In addition, the temples were themselves major employers, owning large tracts of farmland and pasture, flocks, and herds that supplied the temple offerings. Over time, the economic power of the most

*text continues on page 66*

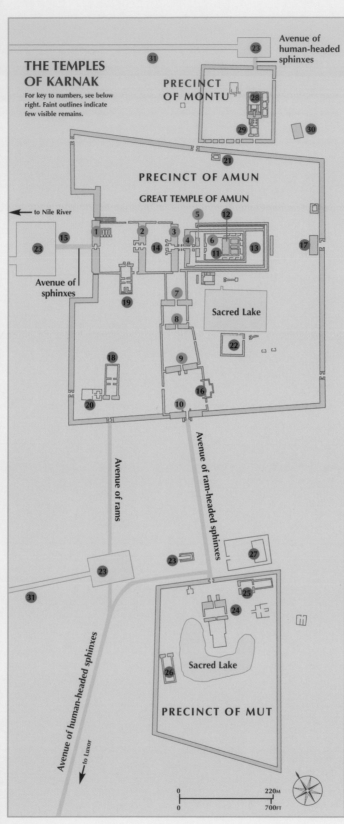

**THE TEMPLES OF KARNAK**

For key to numbers, see below right. Faint outlines indicate few visible remains.

Avenue of human-headed sphinxes

**PRECINCT OF MONTU**

**PRECINCT OF AMUN**

**GREAT TEMPLE OF AMUN**

→ to Nile River

Avenue of sphinxes

Sacred Lake

Avenue of rams

Avenue of ram-headed sphinxes

Avenue of human-headed sphinxes

to Luxor →

Sacred Lake

**PRECINCT OF MUT**

0        220M
0        700FT

**OPPOSITE**

The great temple of Amun at Karnak, looking east. In the foreground is the 1st Pylon, which was in fact the last to be built (probably by Nectanebo I in the 4th century BCE) and was left incomplete. Behind it, between the 2nd and 3rd Pylons, is the Great Hypostyle Hall, and beyond that the remains of three more pylons leading to the sanctuary area, the oldest part of Karnak.

**KEY TO PLAN, LEFT:**

1. 1st Pylon (Nectanebo I)
2. 2nd Pylon (19th Dynasty)
3. 3rd Pylon (Amenhotep III)
4. 4th Pylon (Thutmose I)
5. 5th Pylon (Thutmose III)
6. 6th Pylon (Thutmose I)
7. 7th Pylon (Thutmose III)
8. 8th Pylon (Hatshepsut)
9. 9th Pylon (Horemheb)
10. 10th Pylon (Amenhotep
11. Inner sanctuary (Middle Kingdom)
12. Central court (Middle Kingdom)
13. Jubilee festival hall (Thutmose III)
14. Great Hypostyle Hall (Sety I and Ramesses II)
15. Departure quay for the Barque of Amun
16. Jubilee temple (Amenhotep II)
17. Temple of Amun-Ra Who Hears Petitions (Ramesses II)
18. Temple of Khonsu (20th Dynasty)
19. Temple of Ramesses III
20. Temple of Opet
21. Temple of Ptah
22. Enclosure for sacred fowl
23. Temple harbors
24. Temple of Mut
25. Temple of Khonsu the Child
26. Temple of Ramesses III
27. Temple of Amun Kamutef ("Bull of his Mother")
28. Temple of Montu
29. Temple of Maat
30. Temple of Thutmose I
31. Canals

important temples allowed their priesthoods to wield considerable political power, while the practice of making temple appointments hereditary led to the emergence of influential priestly dynasties.

Karnak, the chief cult center of Amun, was the most important institution of ancient Thebes and the focus of the city's life. Extending over approximately 1 sq mile (2.5 sq km), the Karnak temples comprise three sacred precincts. The central precinct, dedicated to Amun, was the largest and most significant; in addition to the great temple of Amun, it included shrines and temples dedicated to other major gods and goddesses. To the north of the Amun complex is the precinct of Montu, the Theban war god, and to the south, the precinct of the goddess Mut, Amun's consort.

The monuments within the precinct of Amun span a period of more than two millennia, from the Middle Kingdom to the Ptolemaic and Roman periods, although there may well have been older religious structures at the site. During this time, the great temple of Amun was extended and embellished on countless occasions. The main axis of the temple was oriented east-west, facing the Nile and aligned with the daily path of the sun. In the New Kingdom, a new north-south axis was created to form a processional route linking the temple with the precinct of Mut and the temple of Luxor to the south. Over time, the complex expanded along these two axes.

The traditional elements of a temple were the sanctuary (the most sacred part, housing the sacred image of the deity), which was preceded by one or more hypostyle (columned) halls, a peristyle (colonnaded) court, and a pylon (monumental

gateway). Frequently, the temple was extended by the addition of further pylons, which provided a conspicuous public display of the king's devotion while conveniently obscuring his predecessors' monuments. A number of rulers added pylons to the temple of Amun: the spaces created between them were converted into courtyards, or, in the case of the space between the 2nd and 3rd Pylons, a hypostyle hall. The latest part of the temple, the 1st Pylon, created a court that enclosed two structures formerly outside the temple: a small temple of Ramesses III and a chapel of Sety II.

Even those who were not directly involved with the temple as priests or employees would have visited Karnak on business or to participate in the great festivals that punctuated the Theban year. Laypeople were excluded from the temple's sacred precincts, but they had ample opportunity to participate in divine worship at festival times, when the cult images of Amun and Karnak's other gods and goddesses were brought out from their sanctuaries in ritual procession, carried aloft in models of divine boats.

The two main Theban festivals were Opet in summer and the Beautiful Festival of the Valley in spring. During Opet, which lasted two to four weeks, the images of Amun, his wife Mut, and their son Khonsu were taken to Luxor temple, Amun's "Southern Harem," where secret rituals to renew the king's power were conducted. In the Beautiful Festival of the Valley, the deities, borne in magnificent gilded barges, crossed the Nile to the mortuary temples of the kings, accompanied by the population of Thebes, which visited the cemeteries to feast at the tombs of their ancestors.

**ABOVE**
Thutmose III erected these two unique heraldic granite pillars between his 6th Pylon and the sanctuary of Karnak. They bear beautiful reliefs of the lotus, or water lily (foreground), and papyrus, the emblems of Upper and Lower Egypt respectively, and symbolize the unity of the Two Lands. The statue to their left represents Tutankhamun as the god Amun.

# THE HERO KING
## AMENHOTEP II (c.1427–c.1400 BCE)

In the last years of his life, and perhaps with his own history in mind, Thutmose III made his son Amenhotep II his co-ruler in order to secure the succession. Raised at Memphis, Amenhotep was a keen sportsman and hunter who, on a stela which he erected next to the Great Sphinx of Giza, boasted of his military, equestrian, and athletic prowess: "He was one who knew all the works of [the war god] Montu; he had no equal upon the battlefield. He was one who knew horses; in this numerous army there was no match for him. Not one among them could draw his bow; he could not be approached at running."

Like his illustrious father, Amenhotep was a ruthless warrior. When, early in his reign, a coalition of Syrian states rebelled against Egyptian rule, he was swift to crush the revolt, returning to Egypt with the rebel leaders' corpses hung upside-down from the prow of his ship. Six of the bodies were exhibited on the walls of Thebes; the seventh was taken to Napata in Nubia and hung on the city walls as a warning to any would-be rebels in Egypt's African domains.

Amenhotep II also followed his predecessors in erecting a number of temples at Thebes, including a royal Jubilee (Heb-Sed) temple at Karnak and a mortuary temple on the Nile's west bank. However, Amenhotep's finest monument is his impressive tomb in the Valley of the Kings (KV35). Its design is similar to the tomb of Thutmose III, although the burial chamber is on two levels, and is rectangular rather than oval. As in his father's tomb, the wall decoration is executed in the cursive style seen on funeral papyri; however, on the pillars supporting the ceiling there are, for the first time, fully drawn figures of the king with funerary deities. The texts themselves are of great importance as they contain a complete version of the *Amduat*.

When the tomb was excavated by Victor Loret in 1898, the king's mummy was still within its granite sarcophagus, inside a replacement coffin and adorned with garlands of flowers. Two of the storerooms off the burial chamber were found to contain a cache of other royal mummies, including in one chamber Thutmose

**OPPOSITE**
Amenhotep II's burial chamber contains the first fully drawn figures in any of the Valley of the Kings' royal tombs. Here, the deceased king (right) stands before the god Osiris, lord of the dead, who restores him to life, indicated by the *ankh* "life" hieroglyph before the king's face. According to convention Osiris is depicted as a royal mummy: he wears the White Crown of Upper Egypt and holds the royal regalia of crook, flail, and long *was* scepter, an emblem of royal power.

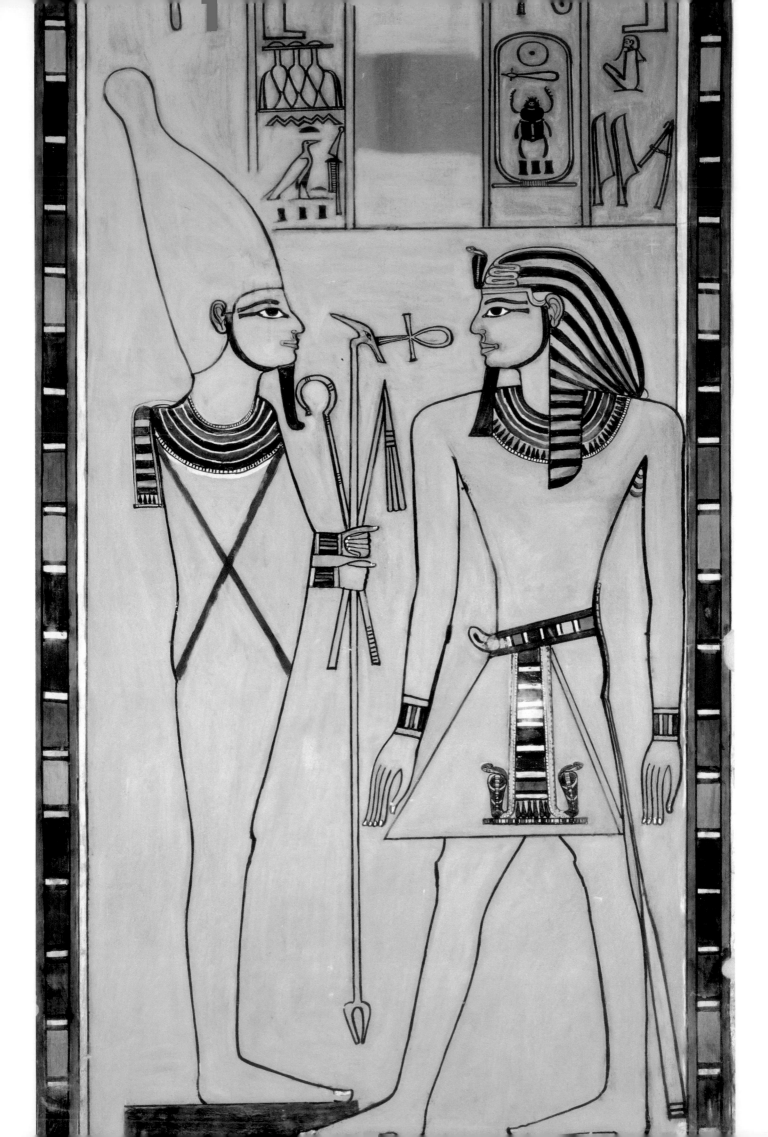

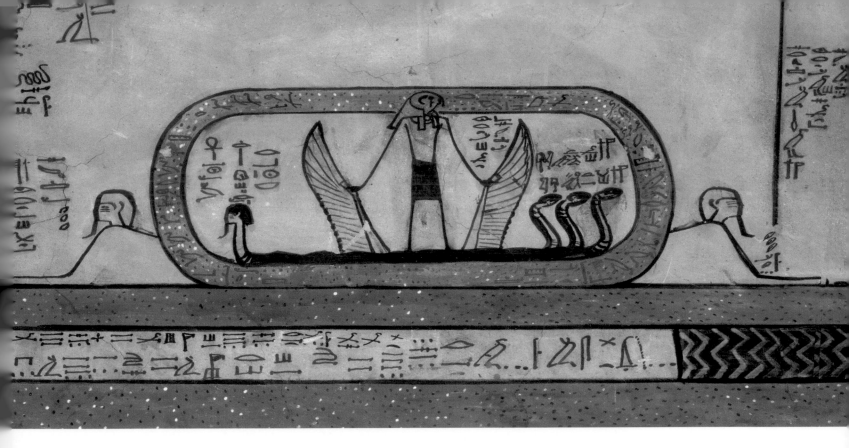

IV, Amenhotep III, Ramesses III, and five other New Kingdom pharaohs, and in a second chamber two women and a boy. All had been stripped of their treasures and some had been reburied in different coffins, indicating the work of robbers. It was proposed in the 1970s that one of the women is Queen Tiye. Members of a recent expedition have suggested that the boy is Prince Thutmose, the eldest son of Amenhotep III, and that the second woman is Queen Nefertiti, principal consort of Akhenaten.

The prosperity of Thebes during the reign of Amenhotep II is reflected in the splendid monuments of his high officials, the most senior of whom were granted the privilege of erecting their own statuary within the sacred precincts of the gods' temples. They included Sennefer, mayor of Thebes under Amenhotep II, and his wife, the royal nurse Sennay, who were both intimates of the royal family and proudly displayed their elevated status in a family statue found in the temple of Amun at Karnak. The figure of Sennefer, adorned with his official insignia and royal gifts of jewelry, is represented with rolls of body fat, an artistic convention often employed in private portraiture to indicate the owner's health and prosperity. The granite statue is unusual in bearing the names of the sculptors who made it, Amenmes and Djedkhonsu.

While the tombs of high officials at Thebes normally had painted chapels where prayers and offerings were made to the spirits of the dead, the underground burial chamber was generally left undecorated. However, Sennefer's tomb at Sheikh Abd el-Qurna has a painted burial chamber, its undulating ceiling decorated with a pattern of entwined grapevines

**ABOVE**
This detail from the *Amduat* in the tomb of Amenhotep II shows part of the underworld's Fifth Hour (of twelve in all), presided over by the hawk-headed funerary god Sokar. He stands between the wings of a serpent with three heads and a tail ending in a human head. The oval represents the wall of sand around the god's "Hidden Land," guarded by the double-headed god Aker.

**OPPOSITE**
The quartzite sarcophagus of Amenhotep II in his burial chamber where Loret found it in 1898, still containing the king's mummy. Its painted sunk reliefs of funerary deities, such as the kneeling Isis (on the end nearest the camera) and the sons of Horus, retain much of their original color. The painted pillars depict the king with the goddess Hathor.

A view of the four-pillared burial chamber in TT96, the tomb of Sennefer, mayor of Thebes under Amenhotep II. The figure of Sennefer appears all around the tomb in the company of his wife and family and the gods. On the pillar on the right, Sennefer and his wife are shown beneath a pair of protective *wedjat* eyes (representing the eyes of Horus), which flank a *djed* pilar, the symbol of Osiris. On the pillar on the left, Sennefer is depicted smelling a lotus (water lily) in several scenes, symbolizing his rejuvenation after death. In the part of the chamber seen here the grapevine design of the ceiling has given way to a colorful geometric pattern representing decorative textiles.

# SECURING THE PEACE
## THUTMOSE IV (c.1400–c.1390 BCE)

**OPPOSITE**

Wall paintings from the Theban tomb (TT36) of the finance minister Sobekhotep depict envoys from Near Eastern vassal states presenting tribute—including gold and ivory—to Thutmose IV. Their characteristic "Syrian" robes, hairstyles, and beards follow Egyptian artistic convention for the depiction of Asiatics.

**BELOW, RIGHT**

Standing between the front paws of the Great Sphinx, the 12-feet (3.7 m) high "Dream Stela" records that Thutmose IV erected it in the first year of his reign. The Sphinx was then already more than 1,000 years old; it is probably an image of the 4th-Dynasty king Khafre (ruled c.2558–c.2532BCE), and forms part of his pyramid complex. In the New Kingdom the monument was identified with Horemakhet (Horus in the Horizon), a solar god.

Among the bodies recovered from the tomb of Amenhotep II was that of his successor, Thutmose IV. Thutmose was not the eldest of Amenhotep's sons, and precisely how he became his father's heir is unclear. Thutmose himself explained this apparent anomaly with an account of a mystical intervention by the solar god Horemakhet, personified by the Great Sphinx at Giza, one of the ancient royal cemeteries of Memphis. According to an inscribed stela that still stands in front of the Sphinx, the god had spoken to Thutmose in a dream "as a father speaks to his son" while the prince had rested in its shadow during a desert hunting trip. The Sphinx promised him that he would one day become king if he cleared the sand that had accumulated around its body. Prince Thutmose followed the Sphinx's instructions and, despite having at least one elder brother, he did indeed succeed his father as pharaoh, although the exact circumstances of his accession are not known.

Thutmose's devotion to Horemakhet reflected a renewed royal allegiance to the solar deities venerated by Egypt's first rulers, but he also maintained the Theban tradition of dedicating monuments to Amun. At Karnak, he constructed a courtyard and an alabaster shrine for the divine barque of Amun. He also erected an obelisk originally commissioned by his grandfather Thutmose III; the tallest ever raised in Egypt, it was removed by the Romans in the 4th century CE and now stands outside the basilica of St. John Lateran in Rome.

The public monuments of Thutmose IV presented him in the same mold as his father and grandfather, as a sportsman and warrior. His prowess was to be tested to the full in a series of campaigns in Nubia and Syria-Palestine. Paintings in the tomb of one of his generals, Tjanuny, depict ranks of Nubian soldiers, while another scene in the tomb of the overseer of the treasury, Sobekhotep, shows the envoys of Syrian vassal states bringing tribute to the Egyptian court (see page 75).

In the latter part of his reign, Thutmose IV adopted a more conciliatory attitude towards his neighbors: one official of Nubian descent, the fanbearer Maiherpri, was granted the extraordinary privilege of a tomb in the Valley of the Kings. This largely intact tomb (KV36) was discovered in 1899 by Victor Loret. Thutmose IV also signed a peace treaty with the Syrian kingdom of Mittani in response to the growing power of the Hittites, sealing the pact with a diplomatic marriage between himself and the daughter of the Mittanian king Artatama I.

The tomb of Thutmose IV is similar in plan to those of his predecessors, but marked a new departure in royal tomb decoration. Instead of the muted hues and cursive style seen in the tombs of Thutmose III and Amenhotep II, the well room and antechamber are decorated with fully formed and brightly colored figures showing the king with funerary deities. Whether this scheme would have extended into the burial chamber is unknown, since Thutmose's early death meant that it was never decorated.

Thutmose was accompanied in death by two of his children, a son and daughter who had died around the same time as their father. The royal mummies were, naturally, buried with the full complement of royal funerary offerings—food and drink, clothes, cosmetics, jewelry, furniture, and even the king's chariot. However, these goods did not remain undisturbed for long, because the tomb was robbed just 80 years after Thutmose's death. The damage was repaired, but following a second robbery Thutmose IV's mummy was removed to KV35, the tomb of Amenhotep II.

**OPPOSITE, ABOVE**
A detail of the hieroglyphic inscriptions and images on the sarcophagus of Thutmose IV. Shown here are (left to right) the gods Hapi, Anubis, Duamutef, and Horus. Hapi and Duamutef are two of the four "Sons of Horus," guardian deities of the deceased's internal organs. The other two Sons of Horus, Qebsenuef and Imsety, are represented on the other side of the sarcophagus.

**OPPOSITE, BELOW**
The fully drawn and brightly painted images in KV43, the tomb of Thutmose IV, were only partly completed in the well room and antechamber. Here the deceased king is shown receiving the breath of life (represented by the *ankh* symbol) from Anubis, the god of mummification, and again from the goddess Hathor, who, as the "Lady of the West," welcomes the deceased to the afterworld. To their left in this detail stands the god Osiris, ruler of the land of the dead.

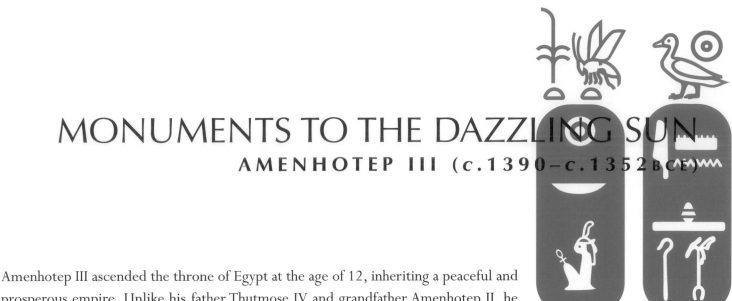

# MONUMENTS TO THE DAZZLING SUN
## AMENHOTEP III (c.1390–c.1352 BCE)

Amenhotep III ascended the throne of Egypt at the age of 12, inheriting a peaceful and prosperous empire. Unlike his father Thutmose IV and grandfather Amenhotep II, he had no need to take an active interest in military affairs; apart from subduing a revolt in Nubia in the fifth year of his reign, he was content to maintain the empire through diplomacy. Some of his dealings with other monarchs are recorded in a remarkable archive of tablets discovered at Amarna in a building called the "Office of the King's Letters." They record how, like his father, Amenhotep III contracted diplomatic marriages with the daughters of his foreign allies, and encouraged them to send their sons to be educated at the Egyptian court. The letters are fascinating and not always diplomatic in tone. In one exchange, the king of Babylon complains that all the foreign kings who have married his daughters have sent him gifts, but Amenhotep, married to the Babylonian king's sister, has sent nothing. Amenhotep replies that he will gladly send the king a gift, then adds tersely: "But it's a fine thing to give away your daughters for the sake of a nugget of gold from your neighbors!"

The reign of Amenhotep III was a period of unprecedented wealth for Egypt, and with the empire at peace, he was able to focus on internal affairs, initiating a large program of rebuilding and renewal. On the east bank at Thebes, he expanded the temple of Amun at Karnak, erecting the 3rd Pylon in front of the previous temple entrance, and beginning a new southern gateway, the 10th Pylon. He started work on new temples to Mut, Khonsu, and Montu, and erected an avenue of sphinxes linking the temples of Karnak and Luxor. On the west bank, he constructed a sprawling new royal palace complex at Malkata, as well as a tomb in the West Valley, adjoining the Valley of the Kings, and a vast mortuary temple at Kom el-Hetan.

However, Amenhotep's best preserved monument was at Luxor, on the east bank, where he dismantled existing temple buildings and created a new temple for the rituals of the Opet festival. Luxor was known as Ipet-Swt, Amun's "Southern Harem" (the word "harem" is used in this context in the sense of "private

**OPPOSITE**
The head of a colossal quartzite statue of Amenhotep III from the great solar court of the king's mortuary temple at Kom el-Hetan, western Thebes. He is depicted wearing the red crown of Lower Egypt.

quarters"), and since the time of Hatshepsut the temple there had been the focus of this annual festival, in which the ruler was renewed through a mystical union with Amun-Ra, and reaffirmed as the god's son. Reliefs in the temple's "birth chamber" narrate Amenhotep III's divine conception and birth.

In accordance with convention, Amenhotep III identified himself as the son of Amun, but, like his father and grandfather, he strove at the same time to revive the ancient identification of the king with the sun god. He assumed the title Aten-Tjehen—"Dazzling Sun Disc"—and built a temple to Aten, the deified sun disc, in the northern city of Heliopolis, the ancient center of the Egyptian solar cult. Aper-el, the vizier for Lower Egypt, was appointed high priest of Amenhotep III's new temple while Ramose, the vizier for Upper Egypt became "steward in the mansion of the Aten." This is the first evidence of the cult of the Aten that was to become so marked a feature of the reign of the king's son, Akhenaten. Two of Amenhotep III's architects, twins called Suti and Hor, erected a stela with a hymn of praise to the "Aten of day, creator of all who makes all things live."

One of Amenhotep III's innovations at Luxor was the addition of a "solar court," open to the sky and enclosed on three sides by a colonnade of columns carved to resemble papyrus-bundles. Solar worship, held in the open air, contrasted sharply with the traditional rites of Amun—the "Hidden One"—conducted in the secrecy of the temple's inner chambers, and the inclusion of this court was a clear statement of Amenhotep's reforming intent. Amenhotep III spared no expense in embellishing the new temple, which is described on a stela in his mortuary temple: "It is made of fine sandstone, very wide and great and incredibly beautiful. Its walls are of fine gold, its pavements are of silver, and all its gates are worked with gold." In front of the temple he constructed a lake surrounded with gardens, "planted with all kinds of flowers."

The administration of Amenhotep III's empire and the implementation of his ambitious building projects relied on an army of officials. These included Ramose and Huy, who both at different times held the post of vizier of Upper Egypt, heading the royal government in this region; the viceroy of Kush, Merymose, who governed Nubia on behalf of the king; and Amenhotep, son of Hapu, the "Chief of Royal Works," his royal namesake's chief planner and architect. Members of the royal family were often appointed to official posts: Amenhotep III's father-in-law Yuya was made lieutenant-commander of chariotry in the army, and his brother-in-law Anen was the Second Prophet of Amun (the most senior priest after the high priest) in the temple at Karnak—where Tuya, the king's mother-in-law, also served as a priestess.

Among the privileges that were granted to high officials were estates and titles, and costly gifts of perfumes and jewelry. They were also permitted to construct magnificent tombs in the Theban cemeteries, and the most favored were allowed to erect statues of themselves in temples, so that their souls might participate for eternity in the divine rituals. Paintings in the tombs of Amenhotep III's officials provide colorful glimpses of life in Thebes during his reign, reflecting the prosperity of the age. Unlike royal tombs, where the decorative theme is concerned with the king's

*text continues on page 89*

**ABOVE AND OPPOSITE**
The tomb of Ramose at Sheikh Abd el-Qurna in western Thebes is one of the most beautiful of its time. The exquisite paintings and low reliefs include scenes of Ramose's funeral banquet attended by family members, such as the couple opposite, wearing intricate braided wigs (the women's adorned with a floral headband), rich jewelry, and fine linen.

**PREVIOUS PAGES**
A painted scene in the tomb of Ramose showing funerary goods including cases for *shabti*s (servant figurines), perfume jars, stools and a pair of sandals being borne in procession to his tomb. On the right, women mourners lament the deceased. Despite its rich decoration, Ramose's tomb was unfinished and he was not buried there. Later parts are in the style of Akhenaten, whom Ramose also served as vizier, and it has been speculated that he was buried at Amarna, Akhenaten's new capital.

**ABOVE**
Female guests at the funeral banquet of Nakht, a scribe and an astronomer ("hour priest") of the Amun temple at Karnak, in a painted scene from his tomb (TT52) at Abd el-Qurna in western Thebes. The women's clothes and jewelry are similar to those portrayed in the tomb of Ramose. In his role, Nakht, who lived during the reigns of Thutmose IV and Amenhotep III, was responsible for examining the stars and fixing the most favorable times for important rituals.

**RIGHT**
Paintings that represented the deceased as they hunted birds in the marshes of the Nile were very common in Egyptian private tombs. This scene shows the scribe Nebamun, an official under Amenhotep III, on a papyrus raft or skiff accompanied by his wife and young daughter. Nebamun wields a throwstick while his cat also catches birds. The chaotic flapping and disarray of the waterfowl symbolize the forces of disorder, over which the deceased displays his mastery.

An elaborately decorated
jewel box discovered in
KV46, the tomb of Tuya and
Yuya, the mother and father
of Queen Tiye. The box is
made of gilded wood with
faience and ivory inlay and is
adorned with the names of
Amenhotep III and Tiye. The
lower register of the box has a
design of repeated *was*, *ankh*,
and *neb* signs, meaning "all
life and strength." Discovered
almost intact in 1905 by a
team funded by Theodore
Davis (see page 100), the
tomb of Amenhotep III's
in-laws was found to contain
jewelry and furniture, as
well as the couple's mummies,
gilded coffins and funeral
masks (see also illustrations
on pages 92 and 93).

divine role in the afterlife, paintings in the tombs of wealthy individuals were intended to provide the deceased with the necessities for life in the next world, and to preserve their privileged lifestyle and status: typical scenes represent the tomb owner engaging in his official duties, relaxing with his family, and participating in leisure activities such as hunting and fishing on the Nile.

During his 38-year reign, Amenhotep III celebrated three Jubilee (Heb-Sed) festivals. These were held at his new Theban palace at Malkata, on the west bank of the Nile, which became the chief royal residence in the last years of the king's life. It has been suggested that Amenhotep III's unconventional choice of location—on the far bank of the river, at the opposite end of the city from Karnak—was made in a deliberate attempt to distance himself from the increasingly powerful priests of Amun.

**ABOVE**
A beautiful miniature head of Queen Tiye, carved in Cypriot yew with obsidian, ebony, and alabaster inlays for the eyes and gold and lapis lazuli ear rings. The queen originally wore a silver and gold headdress (remains of which are visible over her brow) that suggests that the sculpture portrayed her as a goddess protecting her deceased husband Amenhotep III.

The palace at Malkata was built mostly of mudbrick and is now largely ruined, but its scale, together with fragments of the painted plaster decoration and tiled floors from the royal apartments, offer tantalizing glimpses of the opulence of court life. Known as "Splendor of the Aten," the palace was an enormous, sprawling complex of residential buildings, temples, and state apartments, with separate service areas and staff accommodation. On-site workshops supplied extravagant furniture, statuary, and household items, and a vast harbor, connected to the Nile by a canal, sheltered Amenhotep III's magnificent golden state barge, the *Dazzling Aten*.

The palace included suites of apartments for the many members of Amenhotep III's extended family, including his mother Mutemwia; his principal queen, Tiye, and her immediate family; and over 600 minor wives and their children. One of the most remarkable women in Egyptian history, Tiye was married to Amenhotep III shortly after his succession, when they were both aged around 12. As the Great Royal Wife, she was regarded as the king's divine consort, a living goddess essential to the maintenance of divine order in the state and the cosmos, and to the continuation of the divine royal lineage. Tiye and Amenhotep III had two sons, Thutmose and Amenhotep (later Amenhotep IV), and five daughters. The queen took an active role in political life, corresponding on her own behalf with foreign dignitaries.

Amenhotep III's mortuary temple at Kom el-Hetan on the west bank of the Nile was the largest ever erected in Thebes—bigger even, it is thought, than the great temple of Amun at Karnak. As at Luxor, Amenhotep's architects introduced a number of innovative features, including a solar court. In addition, they chose a site on low-lying ground, connected by a causeway to the palace at Malkata. This meant that parts of the temple were flooded during the Nile inundation; as the waters receded, the temple would reemerge, like the primeval mound from the waters of chaos in the Egyptian creation myth, in a symbolic act of rebirth. Amenhotep III's temple is also remarkable for the extraordinary quantity of sculptures with which it was furnished. In addition to a

**ABOVE AND OPPOSITE**
The gilded cartonnage
mummy mask of Tuya and
(opposite) the gilded coffin
of her husband Yuya, from
their tomb. The mummies of
these senior members of the
royal family are among the
best preserved yet to have
been discovered.

number of colossal statues of Amenhotep III himself, there were numerous figures of deities, including jackal-headed sphinxes and over 700 statues of the Memphite goddess Sekhmet. Many of these were subsequently removed and reused by later kings in their own monuments.

Built in the last decade of Amenhotep III's reign, the mortuary temple had already fallen into decay by Ramesside times, when its stone blocks were quarried and reused in the mortuary temple of Merneptah. The temple's floodplain location meant that it was constantly undermined by successive Nile floods, damage that was compounded by a series of earthquakes. Today, little survives of Amenhotep III's vast temple apart from the so-called Colossi of Memnon, a pair of huge statues of Amenhotep that originally fronted the entrance pylon.

Amenhotep III is thought to have died at Malkata shortly before his 50th birthday, and was buried in a tomb in the Western Valley, a branch of the Valley of the Kings. His tomb was of a similar design to those of his predecessors, with the exception of two large chambers adjoining the burial chamber, which may have been intended for the burials of Queen Tiye and his eldest daughter Sitamun. However, the tomb was robbed in antiquity, and its bodies reinterred elsewhere: the mummies of Amenhotep III and a royal woman some have identified as Tiye were among those discovered in KV35, the tomb of his grandfather Amenhotep II, in 1898 by Victor Loret.

Despite the loss of Amenhotep's burial goods, some idea of the wealth lavished on royal tomb equipment at this date can be gained from the treasures in the tomb of his grandson Tutankhamun, and from the tomb of Tiye's parents, Yuya and Tuya, who were granted the privilege of a burial in the Valley of the Kings.

# A TIME OF HERESY
## AMENHOTEP IV/AKHENATEN (c.1352–c.1336 BCE)

One of the most enigmatic figures of Egyptian history, Akhenaten came to the throne as Amenhotep IV, but soon proved to have inherited his father's devotion to the sun god Aten. Within five years of his accession the new king had changed his name from Amenhotep ("Amun is Satisfied") to Akhenaten ("Effective Spirit of Aten").

Amenhotep III had taken care to placate the powerful priests of Amun while pursuing his religious reforms, but his son was more confrontational in his promotion of the cult of Aten. One of Amenhotep IV's first acts as king was to build a great temple of Aten close to the temple of Amun at Karnak. Significantly, the new temple faced east, toward the sunrise, rather than west, toward Amun's sanctuary—almost as if the king himself was turning his back on the traditional god of Thebes.

As hostility between the throne and the priesthood of Amun grew, Akhenaten ordered the construction of a new capital, Akhetaten ("Horizon of Aten") on virgin soil at Tell el-Amarna, over 250 miles (400 km) to the north. A few years after building began, the king and his court abandoned Thebes and moved to the new city. Shortly thereafter, Akhenaten began to suppress the cult of Amun, and most of the other traditional gods and goddesses of Egypt. The names and images of Amun were removed from all public buildings: there was to be only one principal god—Aten—and Akhenaten was his sole intermediary. In public and in private, the new focus of worship was the image of the royal family receiving blessings from the divine solar disc. For Akhenaten and his family, the god Aten encompassed the creative and nurturing forces of the cosmos within a single deity. In royal art, the sun disc hovers above their heads, extending its rays towards them in blessing; each ray ends in a tiny hand holding an *ankh*, the hieroglyph for "life."

Akhenaten's rejection of the traditional roles of kingship also impacted on Egypt's national status. Isolated in his new capital, he took little interest in foreign affairs—a collection of diplomatic correspondence found at Akhetaten paints a picture of a crumbling empire. Many of the letters are from allies pleading for military support

**OPPOSITE**
The head of a colossal statue of Amenhotep IV from the Aten temple at Karnak. The worship of Aten differed from traditional Egyptian temple ritual in that offering rites were conducted in the open air in "solar courts." The focus of the Aten temple was a large open court with an altar, lined with colossi of the king. Erected early in Akhenaten's reign, this statue already displays the striking characteristics of the "Amarna style," notable for its elongated forms and exaggerated flowing outlines, and contrasting sharply with the traditional Egyptian canon of representation.

Reliefs from the Aten temple at Karnak show the royal family standing, hands raised in prayer, as they receive the blessing of Aten's rays. It has been suggested that Akhenaten's androgynous appearance was a deliberate attempt to represent Aten's sole intermediary as both male and female, embodying the divine symbolism of father and mother in one being. When Horemheb demolished the Aten temple he reused its characteristic narrow blocks (*talatat*) as in-fill for new pylons at the adjacent temple of Amun (see pages 123–124). This scene shows Akhenaten followed by Nefertiti in a tall feather crown and is one of a number reconstructed from blocks found inside the 9th Pylon at Karnak.

against enemy attacks: "Let the king take care of his land, and let him send troops. For if no troops come this year, the whole territory of my lord the king will perish."

Details of the events surrounding the end of Akhenaten's reign remain sketchy. In the backlash that followed, his name was excised from public monuments and lists of kings, and official documents subsequently referred to him only as the "Great Criminal." The capital returned to Thebes, and within a few years Akhetaten had been demolished and abandoned.

During the last two years of Akhenaten's reign, the king apparently shared the throne with a shadowy co-ruler, referred to as Neferneferuaten or Smenkhkara. The identity of this figure has been the subject of much speculation; it is generally accepted that the two names belonged to a single person, but it is not clear whether this individual was a man or a woman. It is possible that it was a younger brother of Akhenaten, or perhaps a son, but a more likely candidate is Akhenaten's principal queen, Nefertiti, his childhood bride, who had adopted the title Neferneferuaten early in his reign. She was the chief supporter of his religious and political reforms. The couple had six daughters, but no sons—Tutankhamun was most probably Akhenaten's son by a minor wife. In the absence of an heir, Nefertiti would perhaps have been the figure in whom he placed the greatest trust. From the outset of his reign, the couple had appeared together on Akhenaten's royal monuments, suggesting that she enjoyed rather greater status than was traditionally accorded to the queen.

Akhenaten, Nefertiti, and their children had planned to be buried in the tombs prepared for them in the desert cliffs east of Amarna, but their mummies were probably taken to Thebes when the city was abandoned. One of the female bodies reburied in KV35, the tomb of Amenhotep II, has been ascribed to Nefertiti, but the body of Akhenaten himself has yet to be positively identified. A possible candidate is the royal mummy found in KV55; this tomb contained various items originally from the Amarna tomb of Akhenaten and his mother, Queen Tiye.

# TREASURES OF THE BOY KING
## TUTANKHAMUN (c.1336–c.1327 BCE)

**OPPOSITE**

Ancient Egypt's most famous artifact is surely the gold mummy mask of Tutankhamun. Inlaid with glass and gems, it vividly portrays him as the god Osiris, with whom every dead pharaoh was identified.

**BELOW**

A winged scarab pectoral of gold and precious stones representing the god Khepri, the rising sun, pushing the sun disc above the horizon— spelling out Tutankhamun's throne name, Neb-kheperu-ra ("Lordly Manifestation of Ra").

Within a year or so of Akhenaten's death, a new ruler came to the throne: the nine-year-old Tutankhaten, who is likely to have been the son of Akhenaten by a minor wife. Tutankhaten was married to his elder half-sister Ankhesenpaaten, the daughter of Akhenaten and Nefertiti, in an arrangement that would have helped to confirm his legitimacy to rule. In practice, however, the young king's government was probably controlled by the young king's advisers, the senior courtier Ay, who acted as regent, and the general Horemheb.

Ay and Horemheb—who were both in turn to succeed Tutankhamun as king—are believed to have been the prime movers behind the rapid and thorough suppression of Akhenaten's legacy. The court returned to Thebes, Tutankhaten ("Living Image of Aten") changed his name to Tutankhamun ("Living Image of Amun") and the cult of Amun was restored to preeminence. A stela of Tutankhamun (later usurped by Horemheb) stresses his devotion to Amun and his role in the restoration of the god's cult, and statues at Karnak showed him in the guise of the ancient Theban gods: Amun, Montu, and Khonsu.

Little now remains of Tutankhamun's monuments at Thebes: so thorough was the campaign to eliminate Akhenaten's memory that his son's name, too, was removed from official records, while his statues were usurped by later rulers. However, temple reliefs from Karnak and Luxor, executed in the distinctive Amarna style, indicate that Tutankhamun was as active a builder as his predecessors. Notable among these are relief scenes of the great Theban festival of Opet that flank the processional colonnade in Luxor temple.

The end of Tutankhamun's reign is as enigmatic as its beginning: he died in his ninth year on the throne, at the age of just 18. There has been much speculation as to whether his death, apparently

**RIGHT**
Tutankhamun's beautiful red quartzite sarcophagus is dominated by high relief carvings of the goddesses Isis, Nephthys (right), Neith, and Selket (Serket), who stand at each corner and stretch protective wings over the body of the king. Other amuletic symbols include a *wedjat*, or Eye of Horus, seen here to the right of the goddess. The massive sarcophagus was not removed from the tomb but remains on display in the king's burial chamber, together with the outermost of the three nested coffins that it originally contained (opposite). Inside this gilded coffin the mummy of Tutankhamun lies where it was interred more than 3,000 years ago.

**ABOVE AND FOLLOWING PAGES** On the west wall of the burial chamber (above) a version of the *Amduat* shows the reborn sun god, in the form of a scarab on his barque. Below are listed the 12 divisions (Hours) of the night, each occupied by the figure of a baboon. The north wall (overleaf) shows Tutankhamun, newly restored to life, before the sky goddess Nut (right) and being presented by his *ka* to the god Osiris (left).

occupant. Behind the door was a corridor blocked with limestone chippings; the filling had been tunneled and refilled in antiquity, suggesting a repair after an attempted robbery. Six days later, with the filling cleared, Carter's team cut an opening through a second sealed door and glimpsed for the first time what he called "wonderful things"—the unbelievable splendor of an intact royal burial.

The discovery of Tutankhamun's tomb created a worldwide sensation, and Carter came under enormous pressure to clear the tomb as quickly as possible. However, realizing the huge significance of his discovery, he was adamant that every one of the thousands of items should be properly numbered, photographed, and conserved—a process that was to take more than ten years.

## ROBBERY—BUT AN INTACT BURIAL

As Tutankhamun's tomb was painstakingly cleared, its layout was slowly revealed. The entrance corridor led into a transverse antechamber containing a jumbled mass of tomb models, funerary furniture, chariots, food offerings, chests of clothing, and other funeral equipment, all disturbed during a failed tomb robbery in antiquity. Behind this room was a small annexe or wing containing necessities for the king's afterlife: jars of wine, flasks of perfume, pots of ointment, baskets of fruit, and domestic furniture—these, too, had been disturbed by the robbers.

At the northern end of the antechamber, two standing figures of Tutankhamun, painted black with gilded details, guarded another sealed doorway (see pages 100 and 101). Beyond was a wall of gold: the outermost of four gilded wooden shrines that enclosed the king's sarcophagus, completely filling the burial chamber. When these had been dismantled, another doorway was revealed: not sealed, but guarded by a figure of the jackal god Anubis, the guardian of the royal cemetery. At the back of this chamber—dubbed the "treasury" by the excavators—was the gilded shrine (see page 118) containing Tutankhamun's alabaster canopic chest. Around it were

*text continues on page 110*

**RIGHT**
In addition to many items of
Tutankhamun's clothing—from
sandals and slippers to 27
gloves and more than 100
linen loincloths—the tomb
included this lifesized model
of Tutankhamun in gesso and
painted wood; it may have
served as a mannequin for
the young king's clothes

**OPPOSITE**
One of four inlaid miniature
gold coffins that contained
Tutankhamun's embalmed
internal organs. In the
inscriptions, the cartouche
containing the royal name
has been altered, indicating
that the coffin, which is just
over 1 foot (31 cm) long, was
originally made for one of
Tutankhamun's predecessors.

**FOLLOWING PAGES**
The face of Tutankhamun's
extraordinary innermost
coffin, fashioned from solid
gold some 1–1.2 inches
(2.5–3 cm) thick and weighing
more than 240 pounds (110
kg). It portrays the king as the
god Osiris, with crook and
flail and curved beard.

**ABOVE AND OPPOSITE**
A painted wooden chest from
the tomb is decorated with
scenes of Tutankhamun
leading his troops to victory
over Egypt's foreign enemies—
Nubians on one side of the
chest (above), Syrians on the
other—who are shown in
utter disarray. In contrast,
the Egyptian troops are in
disciplined ranks (opposite).
The two scenes symbolize the
king's divinely ordained role
as upholder of order against
the forces of chaos.

caskets containing some of the most spectacular of the young king's treasures—his royal jewelry and regalia—together with ritual figures and tomb models. These, too, were in a state of disarray following the tomb robbery. Pieces of jewelry found scattered in the tomb's entrance corridor were probably dropped during the robbers' flight.

There can be little doubt that Tutankhamun's early death was unexpected, as many of the objects in his tomb were originally made for other members of the royal family. It is likely that his intended tomb had not been completed, and that he was buried instead in a much smaller tomb intended for a high official, perhaps the elderly Ay. The unfinished decoration in the tomb also points to a hasty burial. Only the burial chamber had been painted, in an interesting combination of the conventional and Amarna styles.

The tomb was the first Egyptian royal tomb to have been found with a largely intact burial assemblage. Dismantling the nest of shrines containing the king's sarcophagus took Carter's team almost three months. Each was made of cedarwood, overlaid with a modeled gesso surface that had then been gilded and, in some cases, inlaid with bright blue faience (decorated earthenware) or black resin. Between the first and second shrines, a gilded framework supported a fine linen cloth spangled with bronze plaques representing flowers.

## A COFFIN FOR AKHENATEN?

Removal of the shrines revealed Tutankhamun's exquisite quartzite sarcophagus, carved with relief figures of protective goddesses, delicately picked out in color (see page 102). Inside, protected by a linen shroud, was the first of three anthropoid coffins containing the royal mummy. All three represented the king as the god Osiris, his arms crossed over his chest, holding the crook and flail symbolizing kingship. The two outer coffins were

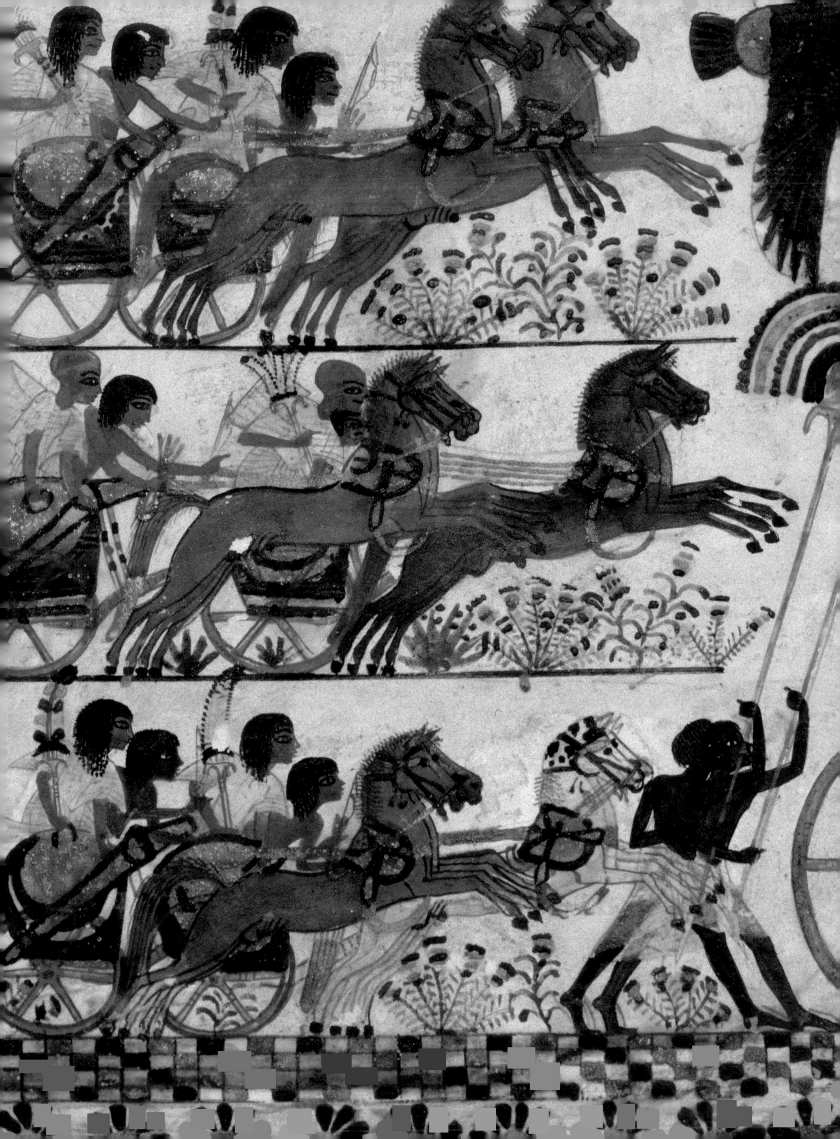

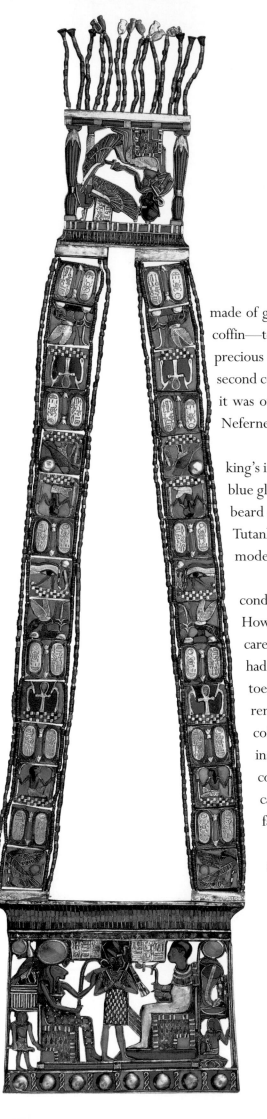

made of gilded wood, the second inlaid with colored glass and faience. The innermost coffin—to the delight and amazement of the excavators—was of solid gold, set with precious stones and colored glass (see pages 108 and 109). The facial features on the second coffin are markedly different from those on the other two, and in all probability it was originally intended for another king, possibly Akhenaten's shadowy successor Neferneferuaten/Smenkhkara (see page 96), or perhaps even Akhenaten himself.

When Tutankhamun's innermost coffin was opened, it revealed the king's intact mummy, with its magnificent solid gold mask (see page 99). Inlaid with blue glass and lapis lazuli, it again shows the king as Osiris, wearing the curved false beard of a god. Nor was the face the only part of the body to be protected this way: Tutankhamun's hands, holding the royal crook and flail, were also provided with a modeled gold cover, sewn on to the mummy wrappings.

Although Tutankhamun's mummy was intact, it was in poor condition due to fungal damage and the excessive application of embalming resins. However, an autopsy confirmed the body as that of a male aged about 18. Great care had been taken over the king's embalming and wrapping: his limbs and digits had been bandaged individually, and gold stalls had been placed over the tips of his toes and fingers. Tutankhamun's lungs, liver, stomach, and intestines had been removed and embalmed separately, then bandaged and put into four miniature coffins of solid gold, inlaid with colored glass and carnelian. These were placed inside alabaster jars, stoppered with portrait heads of the king, which were contained in an alabaster shrine carved with protective goddesses. Again, this canopic equipment was almost certainly made for another member of the royal family, since the names on the miniature coffins have clearly been altered.

Tutankhamun's burial held one further, poignant, surprise: the king's mummy was not the only one in the tomb. Inside the treasury, where his canopic chest rested inside its

**LEFT AND OPPOSITE**
Tutankhamun may have worn these magnificent inlaid gold and silver pectorals at his coronation. The centerpiece of the one on the left is the sun god in the form of a winged scarab. In its claws it grips lotuses and *shen* signs for eternal protection. The god supports a lunar barque, on which *uraei* flank the Left Eye of Horus (the moon) beneath a gold crescent moon and a silver full moon that bears applied gold figures of the king between the moon god Thoth and sun god Horus. The pectoral opposite takes the form of a shrine or temple, in which the king stands between the god Ptah and his consort Sekhmet. Each strap has 15 inlaid gold plaques bearing the royal names and titles and amuletic emblems. On the counterpoise the winged goddess Maat proffers the sign for "life" to the king.

golden shrine, was an undecorated wooden box that held two small coffins, each containing the mummified body of a stillborn baby, probably the children of Tutankhamun and Ankhesenamun.

## A TOMBFUL OF TREASURES

Despite Tutankhamun's short reign, enormous expense was lavished upon his burial. Apart from the golden mask, the king's mummy was adorned with more than 150 magnificent pieces of jewelry, amulets, and regalia. Some of these items were purely ritual in nature, while others would have been worn by Tutankhamun or his predecessors during life. Some of the "reused" items in Tutankhamun's tomb may in fact have been included as "heirlooms." For instance, a small gold figure of a squatting king found inside a miniature coffin is thought to represent his grandfather, Amenhotep III (a lock of hair belonging to his grandmother, Queen Tiye, was found in the same place). Some pieces bear the names of earlier rulers, including Akhenaten and Neferneferuaten; others have been altered, like the miniature coffins holding his internal organs, to include Tutankhamun's names and titles.

## FURNISHING THE AFTERLIFE

Not until the discovery of Tutankhamun's tomb were archaeologists able to obtain a full picture of the quantities of ritual furniture used in Egyptian royal burials. Perhaps the most striking examples from the tomb are the three ritual couches found in the antechamber. Made of gilded wood inlaid with stone, glass, and ivory, each measures about 6 feet (2 m) in length. The sides take the form of pairs of protective animal goddesses: the hippopotamus Ammut, the cow Mehetweret, and the lioness Isismehtet.

An additional 35 ritual figures of gilded wood were also recovered from the tomb. Eight of these represent a king, wearing the regalia of the Two Lands,

in a series of ritual poses; the remainder are figures of protective deities. In addition to these figures was a collection of model boats and a model granary, which were intended to ensure the king's transport and sustenance in the afterlife.

Most numerous among the ritual items in the tomb were Tutankhamun's *shabtis*—small figures of the deceased which, it was believed, would come to life and undertake manual work on his behalf in the afterlife. Private individuals would often be buried with no more than a single *shabti*, but Tutankhamun had no fewer than 413: one worker for each day of the year, plus 36 "weekly overseers" (one for each 10-day Egyptian week) and 12 "monthly overseers" to supervise them. Some of these *shabtis* are clearly female in appearance, and may originally have been made for Neferneferuaten.

In addition to ritual equipment, the deceased king required all the trappings of palace life in order to maintain his status and royal lifestyle in the next world. As in private tombs, the practice of equipping royal tombs with burial goods ensured the preservation of ephemeral articles such as furniture and household items that may otherwise have been destroyed. The furniture from Tutankhamun's tomb covers the whole spectrum of royal furniture, from elaborate ceremonial thrones (see illustrations above and opposite) to the humble folding camp beds and stools used on hunting trips and military expeditions, providing a unique glimpse of court life in ancient Egypt.

**ABOVE AND OPPOSITE**
Tutankhamun's gilded wooden throne displays the style of the Amarna period, notably in the intimate central scene of the king and Queen Ankhesenamun (opposite). This shows signs of alteration: for example, both headdresses cut into the rays of the Aten disc and may be additions. Half of the throne's cartouches retain the names Tutankhaten and Ankhesenpaaten; the rest have been changed to the later forms with the name of Amun.

## THE YOUNG WARRIOR

From the earliest times, the role of the king as warrior was central to the institution of kingship. Akhenaten had been notoriously uninterested in foreign affairs, and Tutankhamun's advisers, keen to present the new king as the restorer of the traditional

BELOW AND OPPOSITE:
The gilded shrine in which the
king's embalmed organs were
contained in miniature coffins.
It is surmounted by two rows
of *uraei* and protected on
each side by the gilded figure
of a funerary goddess (detail
opposite). Shown below are
Isis (left) and Selket.

order, took pains to ensure that, young as he was, he was seen to be actively involved in restoring Egyptian control over its former empire. A painted relief of soldiers from a demolished shrine of Tutankhamun at Karnak represents a victory parade following a successful campaign in Nubia. Whether the young king participated in person is unclear, but his forces make the traditional comparison with the Theban war god Montu: "O Sovereign, you are like Montu, you are like Montu among your army… since you have repulsed him who has arisen in the vile land of Kush."

Many of the objects in Tutankhamun's tomb represent the king defeating Asiatics (peoples of the Levant) and Nubians, Egypt's traditional enemies. They appear on a wooden chest in disarray before the pharaoh's ordered troops (see pages 110–111); they are also represented, as bound captives, on Tutankhamun's footstools, to be trampled by his feet, and on his walking canes. In addition, the tomb contained six chariots, eight shields, and a leather cuirass, together with large quantities of weapons: swords, daggers, bows, arrows, slings, clubs, and throwing sticks.

## THE INTIMATE TUTANKHAMUN

Impressive as Tutankhamun's golden treasures are, perhaps the most fascinating and informative objects from his tomb are the personal items the young king used during his short lifetime. These include his childhood games, his writing materials, his clothes and footwear, his cosmetics, his mirror cases and razor box, his hunting equipment, and his family mementos. Taken together, these humble items, more than any others, grant us an intimate glimpse of the real Tutankhamun.

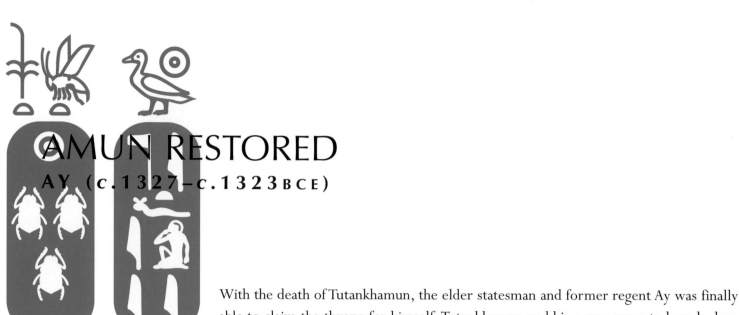

# AMUN RESTORED
## AY (c.1327–c.1323 BCE)

With the death of Tutankhamun, the elder statesman and former regent Ay was finally able to claim the throne for himself. Tutankhamun and his queen seem to have had no surviving children; the two premature stillborn babies buried in Tutankhamun's tomb perhaps suggest that Ankhesenamun may have been unable to carry a child to full term. Ay bore the title "God's Father," which appears to have been based on his status as a senior member of the royal family—it has been suggested that he may have been the father of Nefertiti, or perhaps the brother of Queen Tiye, the wife of Amenhotep III and mother of Akhenaten. Ay probably used this position to legitimize his claim to the succession. Whatever the facts, he clearly had no doubts about his right to rule, since he had himself depicted as king in Tutankhamun's burial chamber.

Ay's brief reign was chiefly dedicated to consolidating the restoration of the cult of Amun. However, if Ay had any hopes that this would earn him the gratitude of posterity they were misplaced, because the family connections that confirmed Ay's succession also ensured that his memory, too, was obliterated after his death. Little now remains of his monuments at Thebes: the paintings in his tomb were defaced, his mortuary temple in the necropolis was usurped by his successor Horemheb, and a chapel at Karnak, dedicated to the memory of Tutankhamun, was demolished by later rulers. Along with Akhenaten and all the other kings associated with the Amarna period, Ay was subsequently omitted from lists of pharaohs of the 18th Dynasty. For example, the list of royal ancestors in the temple of Sety I at Abydos simply skips from Amenhotep III to Horemheb.

Ay's tomb, in the Western Valley (WV23), had probably been intended for Tutankhamun, but was still unfinished even at the time of Ay's death; since the burial chamber proper had not been cut, the antechamber beyond the well room was used instead. The paintings in this improvised burial chamber—very likely by the same artist who decorated Tutankhamun's tomb—are remarkable for juxtaposing the traditional royal funerary texts with a hunting scene normally found only in tombs of the nobility.

**OPPOSITE**
The burial chamber of the tomb of Ay, with the king's restored sarcophagus in the center. The wall paintings of the king before various deities are similar to those in the tomb of Tutankhamun, and are probably by the same artist. However, the images of Ay, together with his name, have been deliberately hacked out, probably as part of a process of eliminating all memory of the Amarna period and the kings associated with it.

# THE GENERAL TAKES CHARGE
## HOREMHEB (c.1323–c.1295 BCE)

The reign of Ay's successor, Horemheb, marked the transition between the Theban 18th Dynasty and the Ramesside 19th Dynasty. He was regarded by his successors as the last king of the 18th Dynasty, and it is possible that he was related by marriage to the royal family—his wife Mutnedjmet may have been the sister of Queen Nefertiti. However, in many ways he can be viewed as the true founder of the 19th Dynasty.

Born at Herakleopolis in the northern Nile Valley, Horemheb first came to prominence as a military commander during the reign of Akhenaten. By the reign of Tutankhamun, he had become the supreme commander of Egypt's military forces and, with Ay, played an important role in the national government. Before he became king, Horemheb built himself an elegant private tomb at Saqqara in the necropolis of Memphis. Reliefs from this tomb show him as a successful young official paying tribute to Egypt's traditional gods and goddesses, and include detailed scenes of his victorious military campaigns on behalf of his king, Tutankhamun.

Much of Horemheb's military career was dedicated to the restoration of Egyptian power in Nubia and the Levant, but after his accession he devoted himself to the reform of the internal administration and to the restoration of religious orthodoxy. The circumstances of his accession are not known, but in the absence of a royal heir, he was probably nominated by Ay as his successor. With a long military and political career already behind him when he came to power, Horemheb went on to enjoy a reign of some 28 years (estimates vary), and he was buried in a splendid tomb in the Valley of the Kings. With no heir of his own, he bequeathed the throne to his vizier, a former military commander, who became Ramesses I, the first king of the 19th Dynasty.

Horemheb completed his eradication of Akhenaten's legacy by ordering the destruction of Akhetaten, Akhenaten's capital, and the demolition of his monuments at Thebes, notably the temples of Aten at Karnak. The dismantled blocks from the Aten temple were reused as filling for Horemheb's pylons in the temple of Amun. Making practical use of demolished monuments in this way had happened

**OPPOSITE**
The painted reliefs in the tomb of Horemheb are among the finest in the Valley of the Kings, although they were unfinished at the king's death. They depict Horemheb with various funerary deities; here he is shown presenting an offering of wine to the goddess Hathor.

before at Karnak, for example with the red quartzite chapel of Hatshepsut (see page 53), but in this case the symbolism of literally burying the Aten cult within that of the newly triumphant Theban god was unlikely to have been lost on Horemheb and his contemporaries. Of the three pylons attributed to Horemheb, only one—the 9th— seems to belong solely to his reign. The 10th Pylon, on the temple's transverse axis, was probably begun by Amenhotep III, while work on the 2nd Pylon, in front of the temple, may have started under Tutankhamun; it was continued by Horemheb and finally completed by his successor, Ramesses I. Horemheb also commissioned an avenue of sphinxes lining the processional way between the temple of Amun and the temple of Mut, but this project, too, was not completed until long after his death.

Apart from his works at Karnak, Horemheb erected few other monuments at Thebes. However, he carried out a wideranging program of usurpation, appropriating the buildings and statuary of earlier kings in his attempts to erase memories of the Amarna period. Most of Tutankhamun's statues and other monuments were reinscribed with Horemheb's name, including the so-called "Restoration Stela" erected at Thebes to commemorate the refurbishment during Tutankhamun's reign of the temples of Egypt's traditional gods, which had been neglected during the Amarna period. Another usurped monument was Horemheb's mortuary temple at Medinet Habu on the Nile's west bank, which had originally been built for Tutankhamun and assumed by Ay.

Although it was never completed, Horemheb's magnificent tomb in the Valley of the Kings (KV57) stands as testimony to his remarkable reign. Its innovative design, while based on the earlier royal tombs in the valley,

**OPPOSITE**
Horemheb completed the restoration of the cult of the god Amun, who is represented in this granite statue protecting the smaller figure of the king. The statue, from Luxor, spells out the king's full name, Horemheb Meryamun ("Horus [the king] Rejoices, Beloved of Amun"). Amun wears his characteristic crown with two tall plumes.

**RIGHT**
This statue of the Theban mother goddess Mut, chief consort of Amun and mother of Khonsu is ascribed to Horemheb's reign. She wears the royal double crown, which relates to her symbolic role (shared with Hathor and Isis) as divine mother of the king. Mut's name was written with the symbol of her sacred bird, the vulture, whose protective wings encircle the headdress.

introduced a number of features that were to become standard in later tombs. Much deeper than the earlier tombs, it has a straight axis rather than a bent one, and a staircase connects the upper and lower levels of the burial chamber. Small chambers adjoining the burial chamber were probably intended for the storage of grave goods.

The tomb was discovered in 1908 by the expedition funded by the American businessman Theodore Davis, whose archaeologist, Edward Ayrton, knew of Horemheb's tomb at Saqqara and was initially surprised to find his royal cartouches in this tomb; but his excavations soon revealed that this was indeed where Horemheb was buried—as king rather than commoner.

When Horemheb died the tomb had clearly been left unfinished—piles of limestone chippings had been hurriedly heaped against the passage walls to allow access to the burial chamber—and later earth movements had damaged the walls and columns. However, many of the colorful painted reliefs—regarded as among the finest in the Valley of the Kings—were in excellent condition. The same could not be said for the contents of the tomb, which had been robbed in antiquity. Apart from a few bones, the king's fine red granite sarcophagus was empty, and fragments of burial goods lay scattered about the floor. These were numerous but in poor condition, and included remnants of animal-shaped couches, model boats, and wooden guardian figures similar to those found in the tomb of Tutankhamun. Also found was the shattered canopic chest and jars for the king's mummified internal organs, remains of which were also found. However, as yet no identifiable remains of Horemheb's mummy have been discovered.

Another innovative feature of Horemheb's tomb was the decision to decorate the walls with carved and painted reliefs; because of the generally poor quality of the limestone in the Theban area, royal tomb decoration had previously been executed on smooth plastered walls. The subject matter was also new: instead of the

**PREVIOUS PAGES**
Painted reliefs in the well
chamber of Horemheb's tomb
(from left): Horemheb offering
wine to the goddess Hathor;
the god Horus leading
Horemheb before the goddess
Isis; and Horus leading
Horemheb before Hathor.

**OPPOSITE**
The goddess Isis, one of the
divine mothers of the king,
wearing a headdress of
cow horns and sun disc. In
Horemheb's tomb the figure
of Isis replaces that of the sky
goddess Nut, who is often
found in earlier royal tombs.

**FOLLOWING PAGES**
An unfinished painted relief
from the *Book of Gates* in the
Horemheb's burial chamber.
The top register depicts the
sun god sailing in his barque
through the second division of
the night; the bottom register
shows prostrate and bound
sinners who face oblivion.

*Amduat*, a new funerary text, the *Book of Gates*, was chosen. Because many scenes were left unfinished, the decorations in Horemheb's tomb provide numerous insights into the practices of ancient Egyptian artists, illustrating all the stages of production from the initial drafting of scenes through carving, plastering, and painting. In contrast to the monochrome paintings found in many of the earlier tombs, those in the tomb of Horemheb were executed in full and vibrant color: in the well room paintings, for example, the figures of the king and the various deities are set against a brilliant blue ground. Even the hieroglyphs are picked out in bright shades. The style of the paintings, too, differs slightly from the very stiff formality of earlier times—a hint of softening that perhaps indicates the influence of Amarna art.

While it appeared to represent a departure from earlier funerary texts, the *Book of Gates* was in fact a development and elaboration of the themes found in the *Amduat*, which narrated the sun god's journey through the underworld during the 12 hours of the night. Its name is taken from the gates that divided the 12 regions of the underworld, each region corresponding to an hour of the night, and its purpose was to enable the deceased king to traverse these regions in safety. The descending corridors of the royal tomb mirrored this journey, in the course of which both the sun and the king negotiated the perils of the underworld to emerge, reborn and renewed, at dawn.

The gateway to each of the underworld regions was guarded by a fearsome snake deity wielding a knife. The second gate was the point where the sun god descended into the underworld aboard his sacred barque, surrounded by protective deities and accompanied by the king. As the sun god passes by, illuminating the dark regions with his brilliant light, the inhabitants of the underworld are seen rejoicing. During the fifth hour of the night, the boat passed the "Secret Cavern of Sokar" containing the Lake of Fire into which wicked souls were cast, never to return. At the midpoint of the journey, the sixth hour, the sun god was reborn, and began his journey to the eastern horizon, where he would reappear at dawn.

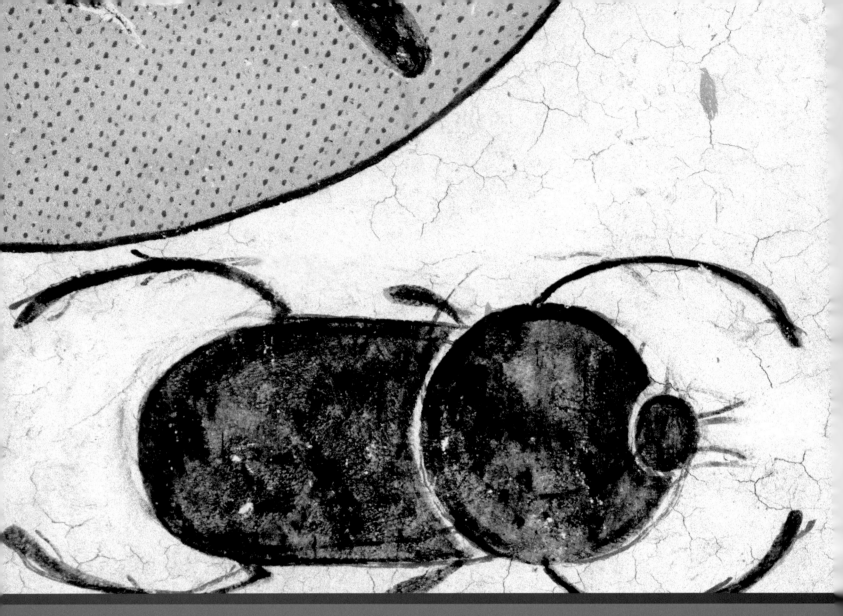

**RAMESSES I**
1295–1294BCE

**SETY I**
1294–1279BCE

**RAMESSES II**
1279–1213BCE

**MERNEPTAH**
1213–1203BCE

**AMENMESSE**
1203–1200BCE

**SETY II**
1200–1194BCE

**SIPTAH**
1194–1188BCE

**RAMESSES VI**
1143–1136BCE

**RAMESSES VII**
1136–1129BCE

**RAMESSES VIII**
1129–1126BCE

**RAMESSES IX**
1126–1108BCE

**RAMESSES X**
1108–1099BCE

**RAMESSES XI**
1099–1069BCE

**WOSRET**
**88–1186**BCE

**SETHNAKHT**
**1186–1184**BCE

**RAMESSES III**
**1184–1153**BCE

**RAMESSES IV**
**1153–1147**BCE

**RAMESSES V**
**1147–1143**BCE

# RULERS IN SOUTHERN HELIOPOLIS

## THE 19TH AND 20TH DYNASTIES (C.1295–C.1069BCE)

# STABILITY AND RENEWAL
## RAMESSES I (C.1295–C.1294 BCE)

Ramesses I, the founder of the 19th Dynasty and the first of eleven rulers to bear his name, was born into a military family from Qantir in the Nile Delta. Little is known of his early career, but he became vizier under Horemheb and thus second in the Egyptian political hierarchy. Toward the end of his life Horemheb appointed him as his heir; given the comparatively recent events of the Amarna years and their aftermath it is unsurprising that both men should have been anxious to minimize the disruption of a reign change.

Ramesses emphasized his determination to ensure political and religious continuity by scrupulously observing royal precedent and tradition. He continued to govern from Memphis, the traditional capital in the north, and erected monuments at many ancient religious sites including Abydos (the cult center of Osiris) and Heliopolis (the cult center of the sun god Ra). At the same time, he took care to uphold the status of Thebes as the focus of state religion and the location of the royal cemeteries. At Karnak, he completed the 2nd Pylon in the temple of Amun: the exterior, covered with reliefs of Ramesses making offerings to Amun and the other deities of the temple, was a powerful public statement of his piety and devotion to the traditional roles of kingship. In the cemetery for royal wives and children in what is now called the Valley of the Queens, located southwest of the Valley of the Kings on the Nile's west bank, the earliest inscribed tomb (QV38) was constructed for one of his queens, Satra.

Ramesses, already elderly at his accession, ruled for less than two years. He did not live long enough to establish a mortuary temple at Thebes, although his son and successor, Sety I, later erected a chapel in his name in his own Theban temple at Qurna on the west bank of the Nile. Ramesses I's tomb in the Valley of the Kings (KV16) was incomplete at the time of his death. Only a small part of the corridor that would have led to the burial chamber was finished; this space was widened to receive the king's sarcophagus and hastily decorated. The scenes echo those in Horemheb's tomb in their style and content, but their coloring introduces the deep yellow hues typical of later royal tomb paintings.

**OPPOSITE**

A painted relief in the burial chamber of KV16, the tomb of Ramesses I, showing the deceased king being protected by Horus, who wears the double crown of Egypt, and Anubis, the jackal-headed god of mummification.

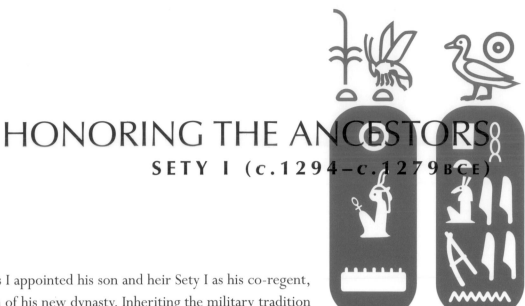

# HONORING THE ANCESTORS
## SETY I (c.1294–c.1279 BCE)

Soon after his accession, Ramesses I appointed his son and heir Sety I as his co-regent, in order to confirm the succession of his new dynasty. Inheriting the military tradition of the family, Sety made his principal concern the consolidation of Egyptian power in the Near East and Africa, and much of his reign was occupied with battling the Hittites and Libyans. His foreign policies secured Egyptian supremacy in the region.

Sety was also an enthusiastic builder. Like his father, he was aware of the political value of building and endowing temples, both in terms of his public image, and—perhaps more importantly—of ensuring the support of the priesthoods at key religious centers. His most famous monument, his memorial temple at Abydos, included a notable relief showing Sety and his son, the future Ramesses II, venerating the names of Egypt's ancient rulers. To underline this respect for royal tradition, the names of "anomalous" rulers such as Hatshepsut and Akhenaten have been omitted from this list.

At Thebes, Sety I renovated the buildings of earlier rulers, and constructed the Great Hypostyle Hall in the temple of Amun at Karnak. In keeping with its public role, the exterior of the northern wall is decorated with carvings of Sety's military victories, the inscriptions attributing his triumphs to the gods. The interior of the hall, more conventionally, shows the king venerating Amun and the other deities of Karnak.

Sety's 15-year reign allowed him more time to prepare his funerary monuments than his father had enjoyed. In addition to his memorial temple at Abydos, he erected a more conventional mortuary temple at Qurna on the west bank of the Nile at Thebes. Sety I was buried in a magnificent tomb in the Valley of the Kings, although his mummy was discovered in 1881 in the royal cache at Deir el-Bahri (DB320), where it had been reburied by the priests of Amun some 200 years after his death. His body—one of the best preserved of all the royal mummies—was found inside its original wooden outer coffin, wrapped in a yellow shroud; a scientific examination revealed that the king had suffered from arteriosclerosis.

**OPPOSITE**
The head of an alabaster statue of Sety I from the temple of Amun at Karnak. The eyes and eyebrows were once inlaid with precious or semiprecious materials, which were removed before the statue was buried in the temple during the Late Period.

**ABOVE**

A relief on the northern exterior wall of the Great Hypostyle Hall of the temple of Amun at Karnak, one of the finest achievements of Egyptian architecture, which was begun by Sety I and completed by his son Ramesses II. It shows Sety I smiting bound captives (who are recognizable as Libyans) before the god Amun.

**OPPOSITE**

The Hypostyle (columned) Hall was created by enclosing the space between the temple of Amun's 2nd and 3rd Pylons and installing 134 massive papyrus-shaped columns. The 12 columns along the central axis are taller, creating a clerestory that allowed light to enter the hall; these 12 represent fully flowering papyrus reeds, while the shorter columns to either side have papyrus-bud capitals like those shown here.

The tomb of Sety I (KV17) is the longest, deepest, and most complete tomb in the Valley of the Kings, and its painted reliefs are among the finest. The design is based on that of earlier royal tombs, with a sloping entrance corridor leading to a well shaft and a pillared hall with an additional chamber. The lower part of the vast, split-level burial chamber is roofed with a magnificent barrel vault painted with celestial imagery; from the floor of the chamber a mysterious passage originally led down to another room that may have had some ritual significance.

Sety's tomb was the first royal tomb to be decorated throughout, from the entrance corridor through to the burial chamber. Whereas normally the long hymn of praise known as the *Litany of Ra* was confined to the burial chamber, here the additional space enabled it to be used throughout the tomb. For the first time, too, the ceiling of the burial chamber was decorated with astronomical scenes including the decans (calendrical divisions of the night sky) and constellations, which are represented as deities.

Many of the finest examples of the funerary papyri referred to today as *Books of the Dead* date from around the reign of Sety I. Reflecting the renewed prosperity of the era, they are not mere texts but fine works of art and calligraphy, written in elegant cursive hieroglyphs and illustrated with exquisite vignettes (miniature paintings). Known to the Egyptians as the *Chapters of Coming Forth by Day*, they were collections of magic spells intended to assist the dead on their journey into the afterlife and to protect them from the dangers of the underworld. About 200 individual spells are known, but no two *Books of the Dead* are identical, because each copy was an individual commission, prepared according to the requirements of the owner, who would specify the spells to be included.

**ABOVE AND OPPOSITE**
The split-level burial chamber of KV17 is decorated with scenes from the *Amduat* and *Book of Gates* and the first "astronomical ceiling." The left of the vault (opposite) shows the decans and their gods (the Egyptians divided the night sky into 36 equal parts, or decans, which rose in turn above the dawn horizon for 10 days a year). The right side of the vault shows stars and star groups of the northern sky (detail above); identification is difficult in most cases, but the bull (opposite, top right) is associated with the constellation we know as the Big Dipper or Plough.

**OVERLEAF**
Sety I's full birth name was Sety Merenptah (He of the god Seth, Beloved of Ptah). The second half of his name is spelled out in this painted relief of the king embracing the creator god Ptah, who is depicted as a mummiform figure wearing an artisan's cap.

The texts in the tombs of the kings narrate the nightly transformation of the sun god, mirroring the daily rising and setting of the sun. However, the *Books of the Dead*, compiled for high-status commoners, are concerned primarily with the mythology of Egypt's other great funerary god, Osiris, and present an alternative image of death and renewal reflecting the agricultural cycle.

Above all else, the purpose of the incantations in the *Books of the Dead* was to ensure that the deceased would be able to find their way to the court of Osiris, where they would be judged worthy to reside in the Egyptian paradise, the Fields of Reeds. This was represented as a rich agricultural region, the estate of Osiris, who ruled over the realm of the dead just as the pharaoh ruled over Egypt. In his judgment hall, before the gods and goddesses of Egypt, the heart of the deceased was weighed against the Feather of Truth (Maat) to ascertain whether the owner was "justified"—worthy of eternal life.

**ABOVE**
This judgment scene from the *Book of the Dead* of the Theban scribe Hunefer (c. 1285BCE) shows the god Anubis weighing the deceased's heart against the Feather of Truth to determine whether he has lived a viruous life. The hearts of those who failed this test were consumed by the "Devourer"—a hybrid of crocodile, lion and hippopotamus—who waits beneath the scales, an act that will deprive the deceased of eternal life.

# RAMESSES THE GREAT
## RAMESSES II (C.1279–C.1213BCE)

**OPPOSITE**
The face of a shattered colossus of Ramesses II at Luxor temple. The self-styled "King of Kings" left his mark on posterity more than any other pharaoh, and his many monuments are to be found throughout Egypt. As well as commissioning new buildings, temples, and statues, Ramesses usurped many of his predecessors', having them recarved with his own name and even, in the case of some statues, with his own features.

**FOLLOWING PAGES**
Ramesses II added a peristyle (colonnaded) court (page 146) and a pylon, or gateway (page 147), to Amenhotep III's temple of Amun at Luxor. Before the pylon, which bears reliefs of the battle of Qadesh, are two colossal seated statues of the king. Ramesses II also erected a pair of obelisks, one of which was removed to Paris in 1819. The processional colonnade erected by Amenhotep III can be seen beyond the entrance.

Ramesses II is, after Tutankhamun, perhaps the most famous king of ancient Egypt, mainly because of the profusion of monuments—both original and usurped—that bear his name, but also because he is often identified as the biblical "Pharaoh" associated with the Hebrew Exodus. In keeping with family tradition, Sety I had appointed his son co-regent toward the end of his life, and accordingly the teenage Ramesses II succeeded to the throne upon Sety's death c.1279BCE. He enjoyed an extraordinarily long reign spanning 67 years and fathered numerous heirs, many of whom predeceased him: he was eventually succeeded by his son Merneptah (see page 164).

Throughout his long rule, Ramesses II's chief concern was the preservation of Egypt's power and prestige in the Near East. He had inherited the family's martial disposition and his new capital, at Piramesse (Qantir) in the eastern Delta, doubled as a military base for his campaigns in Syria and Palestine.

The Hittites, a warlike people of what is now southeastern Turkey, had for some time been expanding their influence into northern Syria, threatening Egyptian interests in the region. In c.1274BCE matters came to a head when the young Ramesses II confronted the Hittite king Muwatallis at the battle of Qadesh, in Syria. Unsurprisingly, the Egyptians represented the battle as a great victory, but in reality it ended in a stalemate that eventually led to a peace treaty. In accordance with ancient precedent, the peace was sealed by a royal marriage between Ramesses II and a Hittite princess.

At home, Egypt prospered thanks to the long peace, as revenues from the empire swelled the state coffers. Like Sety I, Ramesses was a prolific builder, and in addition to completing many of his father's projects, including his mortuary temple at Qurna on the Theban west bank and the Great Hypostyle Hall in the temple of Amun at Karnak, he erected numerous monuments of his own at sites stretching from the Delta in the north to Nubia in the far south. At Thebes he also extended Amenhotep III's Luxor temple, constructed magnificent tombs and mortuary temples for himself and his family, and made many additions of his own to the temple of Amun at Karnak.

Some of Ramesses II's monuments at Thebes fared better than others. His tomb is particularly poorly preserved—it was sited in a geologically unstable part of the Valley of the Kings that was also prone to severe flooding. Paradoxically, Ramesses' mummy is one of the best preserved, having been removed in ancient times to the Deir el-Bahri cache (DB320), where it was interred in a simple wooden coffin stripped of all decoration. Despite this ignominious fate, the 3,000-year-old mummy strikingly conveys the regal dignity of a king who must have been well into his 80s when he died.

Ramesses II was a shrewd statesman, well aware of the importance of his public image. With the capital now in the far-off Delta, the need to cultivate popular support at Thebes was crucial, and in consequence he embarked on an ambitious building program in the city, focussing on the outermost—and therefore most visible—parts of the monuments. He also instituted a thorough program of usurpation, removing the names of previous kings from their monuments and substituting his own.

Having completed decorating his father's Great Hypostyle Hall at Karnak (see page 63), Ramesses stamped his identity on the temple façade, erecting a pair of

colossal statues in front of the 2nd Pylon, which at the time was the entrance. An avenue of ram-headed sphinxes, each protecting a small figure of Ramesses, led from a new quay in the temple harbor, creating an impressive approach to the Precinct of Amun. In a further gesture of popularization, he also added a small temple at the rear of the main one, accessible to the general public and dedicated to Amun-Ra "Who Hears Petitions."

At Luxor, Ramesses extended the temple of Amun by adding a colonnaded court and a pylon to the front of the existing building (see previous pages). Once again, the intention was to create an impressive approach—indelibly stamped with Ramesses' image—to the sanctuary of Amun. Inside, the court is lined with papyrus-bud columns interspersed with standing figures of Ramesses II. In order to align the new entrance with the processional way leading to Karnak, the temple axis had to be altered, and as a result the court is somewhat irregular in plan.

Early in his reign Ramesses II began work on his funerary monuments at Thebes: his tomb in the Valley of the Kings and his mortuary temple, the Ramesseum. Ramesses' monuments are notable for their grandiose scale, and his tomb (KV7), is no exception—the burial chamber alone occupies 1,940 sq feet (81 sq m). Unlike previous royal tombs, it did not have a concealed entrance; instead, a monumental doorway was surmounted with a painted relief of the protector goddesses Isis and Nephthys flanking a solar disc. Originally the interior, too, was decorated, but extensive flood damage in antiquity has left few traces of the once magnificent paintings.

The Ramesseum has also suffered the depredations of time, earthquakes, and quarrying—its masonry was extensively reused for other buildings in ancient times. Nonetheless, it remains one of Ramesses' most impressive and atmospheric monuments (see pages 10 and 17). Built on a site already sanctified by a shrine of his father, Sety I, the complex also included a small mortuary temple for Ramesses' mother, Tuya.

To the south of Ramesses' own temple was a small palace that he used on visits to Thebes for important religious festivals. During a king's lifetime, his mortuary

RIGHT
The Ramesseum, the mortuary temple of Ramesses II, remains impressive despite ancient damage. Among the most striking features of the temple, which was originally named "United with Thebes," are a number of colossal statues of Ramesses II, such as these four figures in the second court of the temple that represent the king as the mummiform god Osiris. In the foreground is the head of another tumbled statue. In the 1st century CE the writer Diodorus Siculus wrongly identified the Ramesseum as the "tomb of Ozymandias" (a Greek version of Usermaatra, Ramesses II's throne name). Shelley's poem *Ozymandias* was partly inspired by the bust (now in the British Museum) from another of the temple's broken colossi. The largest statue of all was a seated figure of Ramesses II that originally stood 58 feet (17.3 m) high.

**ABOVE**
These solid gold bracelets, set with lapis lazuli and bearing the cartouches of Ramesses II, illustrate the opulence of the royal court in Ramesses' time and testify to the skill of ancient Egyptian jewelers. The lapis lazuli forms the central body of a goose, which has two heads and a tail worked in gold. Found in 1906 in the Nile Delta, the bracelets were probably a gift from the king to a favored courtier.

**OPPOSITE**
The upper part of a painted limestone figure of Ramesses II's daughter Meritamun, who became Chief Royal Wife after the death of her mother Nefertari. The object in her hand is a *menat* necklace counterpoise in the form of Hathor, indicating that Meritamun served as a priestess of the goddess.

temple served as the principal cult center of Amun in western Thebes; after his death, it became the cult center of the deceased ruler. While the king lived, therefore, his temple played a central role in the major Theban festivals, especially the annual Beautiful Festival of the Valley, when the sacred images of Amun, Mut, and Khonsu were taken in procession from Karnak to the mortuary temple. This was a great state occasion and required the king to attend in person. After the court's relocation to the north of Egypt at the end of the 18th Dynasty, Ramesses II's father, Sety I, had introduced the practice of building a small palace adjacent to the mortuary temple. This would serve as a temporary residence while the king lived and a home for his spirit after death.

As well as promoting his own name through his many monuments, Ramesses II commemorated his family on an almost unprecedented scale. Devoted to his mother, Tuya, he erected many statues and monuments in her name. He established a large harem of wives and concubines, but his favorite spouse was his childhood bride and Chief Royal Wife, Nefertari, who often appears beside him on his monuments and was buried in a magnificent tomb (QV66) in the Valley of the Queens (see pages 152–155). Perhaps the most beautiful of all Ramesses' Theban monuments, it is simple in design, with a corridor descending to a hall with a subsidiary chamber leading on to the burial chamber. It is decorated throughout with exquisite and richly toned paintings depicting Nefertari with funerary deities and scenes from the *Book of Gates*.

After Nefertari's death the position of Chief Royal Wife passed to a secondary wife, Isetnofret, and then in turn to two of Ramesses' daughters, Bint-Anath

**RIGHT, OPPOSITE, AND FOLLOWING PAGES**
Scenes from QV66, the tomb of Queen Nefertari, the Chief Royal Wife of Ramesses II. When Ernesto Schiaparelli discovered QV66 in 1904 the magnificent paintings were in a pristine state, but by the 1980s they had been badly damaged by salt encrustation caused by rising groundwater. Under the auspices of the Egyptian government, the Getty Conservation Institute has now restored them to their full glory. **RIGHT** Ramesses II (right) in the leopard skin of a *sem* (funerary priest) before Osiris. **OPPOSITE** Wearing an elegant white robe and a vulture headdress surmounted by the twin ostrich feathers and solar disc associated with the god Amun-Ra, the queen is led by the goddess Isis. **FOLLOWING PAGES** Flanked by the ibis-like *benu* bird (phoenix), which represents the sun god, and Heh, the god of infinity, Nefertari's mummy is guarded by the goddesses Isis (right) and Nephthys in the form of two kites.

and Meritamun. Both Ramesses II's sons and daughters appear beside the king on royal monuments. His most famous son—the names of at least 52 are known—was the fourth, named Khaemwaset, the high priest of Ptah at Memphis, who was responsible for restoring ancient royal monuments in the Memphis cemeteries and for endowing the catacombs where the sacred Apis bulls were entombed. Many of Ramesses II's sons were buried in a communal tomb, the largest in the Valley of the Kings (KV5), which was entered in the 19th century but has only been fully explored since its relocation in the mid-1980s. The continuing excavations by Kent Weeks and his team have revealed a remarkable multilevel tomb that may prove to contain more than 150 chambers.

# SERVANTS IN THE PLACE OF TRUTH
## THE TOMBWORKERS' VILLAGE, DEIR EL-MEDINA

**ABOVE**
Tombs of the village elite at Deir el-Medina. They were approached by an open court, sometimes entered by a small pylon. At the far end of the court, a portico marked the entrance to a small funerary chapel surmounted by a mud-brick pyramid (the one in this photograph has been restored). Pyramids were no longer an architectural feature of royal tombs, but remained popular for wealthier private individuals. In the court a concealed pit (seen here in the right fore-ground) led to a vaulted and decorated burial chamber.

Very few places where ordinary Egyptians lived have been preserved in good condition. Because of this, the ancient tombworkers' village at Deir el-Medina ranks among the most important and fascinating sites of Thebes. Hidden in a remote desert valley between the Valley of the Kings and the Valley of the Queens, the village was established in the early 18th Dynasty to house the "Servants in the Place of Truth"—the artists and craftsmen who worked on the royal tombs. It remained in use for nearly 400 years, undergoing considerable expansion during the 19th Dynasty, but was eventually abandoned during the troubled times of the late 20th Dynasty, when its isolated situation made it vulnerable to attacks by Libyan raiders.

Of almost 70 houses in the village, a dozen have been identified as belonging to known families; in some cases their names are painted on the doorposts. Constructed of mudbrick on stone foundations, their basic plan comprises an entrance hall with a raised shrine, a living room with a raised ceiling supported on a wooden column, and a kitchen yard with a clay oven. Stairs led down to cellars for storing valuables and household commodities, and up to the roof, which provided additional sleeping and storage space. The interior walls were plastered and painted, sometimes with colorful geometric designs imitating decorative textiles.

Furnishings in Egyptian homes were sparse and simple; rooms were small and wood scarce and expensive. Clothing, cosmetics, and valuables were stored in baskets, pots, or wooden chests, and meals were served on trays, sometimes supported on portable stands. Wealthier houses had wooden beds, chairs, and stools, but in humbler homes, like those at Deir el-Medina, mudbrick divans in the living areas doubled as places to sit by day and beds at night.

In addition to quantities of personal items found in the tombs at Deir el-Medina, an extraordinary amount of documentation has been recovered in the form

of papyri and also ostraca, flakes of stone and shards of pottery used for casual writing or drawing. These documents include letters, legal documents, songs, stories, sketches, prayers, poems, and even laundry lists, which have enabled scholars to piece together a vivid picture of the villagers' lives.

The workmen of Deir el-Medina spent eight or nine days of the ten-day week away at work in the Valley of the Kings or Valley of the Queens, sleeping in temporary camps and returning home only at weekends. During the week, the village was the province of the women, who enjoyed the luxury of state-supplied domestic help—cleaners and laundrymen allocated to individual households on a rotation system.

Perhaps because of their isolated situation, the villagers formed a very close community, with many intermarriages between families. Outside of their official occupations, members of the community doubled as doctors, letter writers, lawyers, seamstresses, fortune tellers, farmers, and market gardeners, bartering their skills in exchange for goods and services.

**ABOVE**
The tombworkers' village at Deir el-Medina, looking east from the village necropolis toward the Nile floodplain; the Ramesseum can be seen at top left. The village was investigated by Ernesto Schiaparelli from 1905 to 1909 and excavated by Bernard Bruyère, assisted by Jaroslav Cerny, between 1917 and 1947.

The remote location of the village, chosen in an attempt to preserve the secrets of the royal tombs, meant that all the community's needs, including food, water, and clothing, had to be brought up from the valley. On several occasions during the 20th Dynasty, the workmen responded to disruptions in these supplies by leaving their work and marching to local temples to demand payment—perhaps the earliest recorded industrial action. A workers' petition dated to Year 29 of Ramesses III's reign reads: "It is because of hunger and because of thirst that we come here. There is no clothing, no ointment, no fish, no vegetables. Send to Pharaoh our good lord about it, and send to the vizier, our superior, that provision may be made for us."

Religious life at Deir el-Medina revolved around the many festivals of the gods and goddesses; work records from the village suggest that by the late New Kingdom, the villagers were spending about a third of the year preparing for, celebrating, and recovering from these festivities. As elsewhere in Thebes, Amun was regarded as the principal deity of Deir el-Medina, where a small temple to the god had existed from the time of the village's foundation. The villagers also worshiped a number of other deities, including Thoth, the patron god of scribes, and Ptah, the patron god of craftsmen. The goddess Hathor was particularly significant to the community in her funerary aspect as the "Lady of the West," who welcomed the dead to the afterlife, and a small temple dedicated to her stood to the northeast of the village, just outside its walls. The importance of Hathor's cult at Deir el-Medina is demonstrated by the fact that her temple remained in use long after the village itself had been abandoned, and was rebuilt several times—the present temple dates from the Ptolemaic period.

Close to the shrine of Hathor was a temple dedicated to the deified King Amenhotep I and his mother, Queen Ahmose Nefertari. Regarded as the founders of the community, they were the patron deities of Deir el-Medina and small images of the royal

**BELOW AND RIGHT**
Among the many personal items found in the intact tomb of Kha and Merit were a vase for perfume or ointment (right) and a wooden cosmetics chest (below). Kha was overseer of construction at Deir el-Medina under Thutmose III and his son Amenhotep II, who presented Kha with a gilded cubit-rule (also found in the tomb) in recognition of his work.

couple were venerated in household shrines and represented in tombs. The temple of Amenhotep and Ahmose Nefertari was the focus of joyous festivals throughout the year: during their "Great Feast" each winter, the workers and their families, drunk on beer and wine, would make merry before their shrine for four whole days.

Many villagers at Deir el-Medina would have held part-time positions as priests and priestesses in local temples, but in general the public were excluded from the elaborate state temple ceremonies. However, they could bring offerings to the temples, worship divine images in their household shrines, and erect their own modest monuments. Many votive items and stelae requesting divine blessings have been recovered from the precincts of the temple at Deir el-Medina.

Popular religion in the village tended to focus on deities of a more domestic character, such as the god Bes, who was regarded as the protector of women and children, and the household. Magic was another traditional element of popular religion, and charms and amulets were widely used by the villagers to bring good fortune and ward off potential dangers such as bites and stings from poisonous creatures. Another potential danger was from the ghosts of the dead, who, it was believed, could disturb and even harm the living. In order to placate deceased relatives, many homes were equipped with false doors that allowed the spirits of dead family members to visit, while images of ancestors were venerated in special shrines.

160

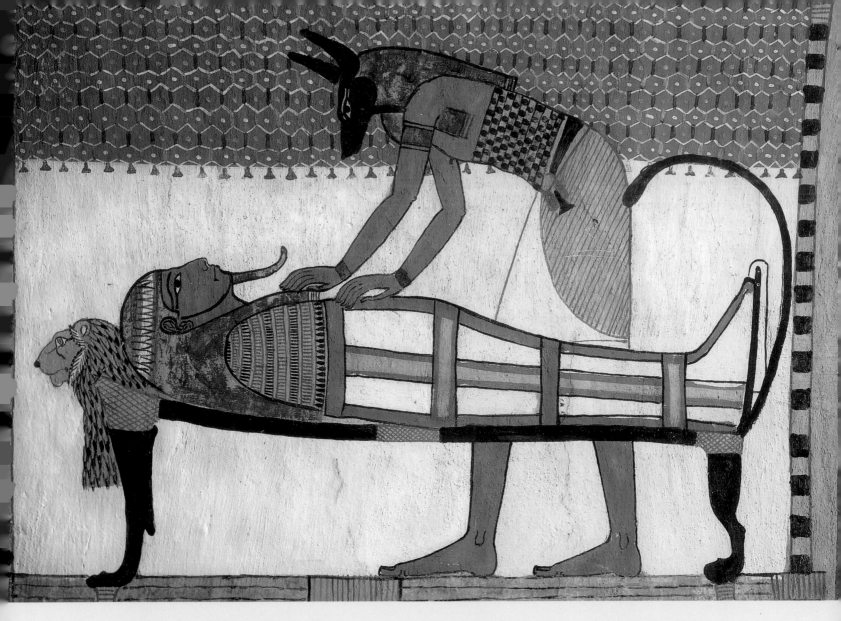

The cemeteries of Deir el-Medina extend along the sides of the valley flanking the village, the tombs of the dead just a short distance from the homes of the living. The distribution of the tombs reflects the community's social divisions, with the elegant tomb chapels of high-status villagers—the work supervisors and government officials—ranged in terraces along the northwest side of the valley, while the humbler workmen were buried in simple pit graves on the opposite side.

Because of their occupation, the villagers were keenly aware of the need to prepare for the afterlife. They were also well placed to equip themselves with burials of the highest quality by bartering their services among the community. Most of this work would have been carried out during the "weekends" when the workforce returned to the village. Unusually for tombs of private citizens (as opposed to those of the royal family), the burial chambers are decorated; even more unusually, the subjects chosen often include mythological scenes clearly inspired by those found in the royal tombs.

**ABOVE AND OVERLEAF**
A painting from the tomb of Sennedjem, an official at Deir el-Medina during the reigns of Sety I and Ramesses II, showing a funerary priest dressed as the god Anubis.

**PAGE 163** The painted door from Sennedjem's burial chamber. The exterior (left) shows him and his family before funerary deities; on the interior (right) he and his wife Iyneferti play the board game *senet*, which may symbolize the journey to eternal life.

# THEBES IN TROUBLED TIMES
## MERNEPTAH (c.1213–c.1203 BCE)

Ramesses II had been on the throne longer than any New Kingdom monarch—indeed, his 67-year reign was the second longest in Egyptian history, being surpassed only by the 94-year rule of Pepy II of the 6th Dynasty a thousand years earlier. During his reign "Ramesses the Great" had established a strong authority that had brought prosperity and peace to Egypt, and he left his throne secure. He had also outlived many of his more than 50 sons, and it was his 13th son, Merneptah, who ascended in his stead.

Merneptah, who was probably in his 60s by the time of his accession, had to contend with periodic invasions of economic migrants seeking land on which to settle. The fertile farmlands of the Nile Delta were an irresistible attraction to both the Libyans, who lived on the desert fringes west of the Delta, and to the "Sea Peoples," a loose confederation of groups from Asia Minor and the islands of the Aegean who had been dispossessed by political events in the Near East. Essentially herders and farmers, both groups made repeated attempts to occupy land in the Delta, and the Egyptians repulsed the invaders only after a long and bitter struggle.

Merneptah's battles against the Sea Peoples are described on a large stela found in his mortuary temple at Thebes that describes the might of the king in dramatic terms: "His victories are assured in all lands, so that every land may see that his conquests are glorious; Merneptah, the Bull, Lord of Power, who slays his foes, beautiful upon the field of victory." This stela is known as the "Israel Stela" because it is the first Egyptian text, and the oldest document outside the Bible, to mention "Israel" among the peoples subject to the pharaoh. It records that "Israel is laid waste, its grain [or "offspring"] does not exist."

During Merneptah's reign Egypt's economy quickened its fall into decline; the prolonged campaigns against the Libyans and Sea Peoples drained the treasury, and the king was forced to control the temple endowments at Thebes. Preoccupied with more pressing matters, he found little time for building projects. At Karnak the only surviving evidence of his reign consists of a copy of the Israel Stela

inscription and a wall enclosing the courtyard of the 7th Pylon; a relief carved on the wall shows Egyptian soldiers breaching the walls of an enemy fortress.

Merneptah's chief Theban monuments are his fine tomb (KV8) in the Valley of the Kings and his mortuary temple on the west bank of the Nile. Hastily constructed using blocks taken from the nearby mortuary temple of Amenhotep III, Merneptah's temple is smaller than those of his predecessors, but similar in design, comprising a central sanctuary preceded by a hypostyle hall and two courts.

Merneptah's tomb is constructed along a single straight axis leading from the entrance passage to the burial chamber. The walls are decorated with scenes from the *Litany of Ra*, the *Book of Gates*, the *Amduat*, and a new funerary text, the *Book of Caverns*. In this last text, the divisions of the night are represented as a series of oval caverns, in which figures of the dead and various deities lie inert, waiting to be revived by the passage of the sun.

In the burial chamber, Merneptah's mummy was laid to rest inside a series of four nesting sarcophagi, three of which survive in part while one is complete (it was later reused by King Psusennes I in the 21st Dynasty). The three outer sarcophagi were of red Aswan granite, while the fourth and innermost was crafted from pale alabaster. These sarcophagi were so large—the outermost was over 17 feet (5 m) long—that the door jambs in the passages and halls of the tomb had to be removed to allow them to be hauled into the burial chamber. Little else of Merneptah's funerary equipment survived ancient floods and tomb robbers. As was the case with his father and grandfather, his mummy was removed in antiquity and reburied, this time in the tomb of Amenhotep II (KV35).

**ABOVE**
A painted granite bust from a colossal seated statue of Merneptah that originally stood in the second court of his mortuary temple at Thebes. The *nemes* headcloth and false beard were traditional elements of an Egyptian king's regalia.

**OPPOSITE**
The burial chamber of KV8. In the center is the restored lid of Merneptah's second granite sarcophagus, sculpted in the shape of a cartouche and portraying the deceased king holding his crook and flail.

# STRUGGLES FOR POWER

## AMENMESSE AND SETY II (c.1203–c.1194 BCE)

Dormant rivalries among the extended family of Ramesses II erupted on the death of Merneptah, when the throne passed not to Merneptah's son, Sety, but to Amenmesse, another grandson of Ramesses II. Little is known of Amenmesse's short reign (c.1203–c.1200BCE), because his name was systematically erased after his death (probably by Sety II) and few inscriptions or monuments survive. Amenmesse's tomb (KV10) in the Valley of the Kings was never completed, and it is not known whether he was ever buried there. However, it was used for the burials of two royal women, Baketweret and Takhet, who may have been Amenmesse's wife and mother. The identities of three mummies found in KV10—two females and a male—have not been confirmed.

On Amenmesse's death, Merneptah's son was at last able to claim the throne. Already elderly, Sety II ruled for just six years (c.1200–c.1194BCE) and seems to have enjoyed a peaceful reign. His modest building program at Thebes included a triple shrine for the sacred barques of Amun, Mut, and Khonsu in front of the temple of Amun at Karnak, and two small obelisks on the temple quay. He planned a double tomb in the Valley of the Kings (KV14) for himself and his queen, Tawosret, but this was eventually occupied by Sethnakht (see pages 170–173). The latter hurriedly decorated an unfinished tomb (KV15) for Sety II and placed his red granite sarcophagus in the unfinished corridor beyond the pillared hall. Sety II's mummy was later removed to the royal cache in KV35, the tomb of Amenhotep II. The decoration in KV15 is mainly traditional (scenes from the *Litany of Ra*, *Amduat*, and *Book of Gates*); however, the well room has unique scenes of the king in a series of ritual attitudes identical to those of the gilded wooden figures found in the tomb of Tutankhamun.

The most spectacular find from the reign is a hoard of jewelry from KV56, the "Gold Tomb." This may have been the burial of one of Sety II's children, or perhaps a place where tomb robbers hid their booty.

**OPPOSITE**
A statue of Sety II from Karnak, showing the king holding a divine standard with the figure of a god.

**BELOW**
Gold earrings bearing the name of Sety II, from the so-called "Gold Tomb" (KV56). Found by Edward Ayrton in 1908, this anonymous tomb—perhaps that of a child of Sety II and Tawosret—yielded some of the finest jewelry ever discovered in the Valley of the Kings, including gold rings, bracelets, earrings, jeweled pendants, amulets, and silver sandals.

# A DECADE OF TRANSITION
## SIPTAH, TAWOSRET, SETHNAKHT (c.1194–c.1184BCE)

It seems that Sety II had two sons, but the elder, named Sety Merneptah after his father, predeceased him, leaving his younger brother Siptah as heir to the throne. On Sety II's death, Siptah (c.1194–c.1188BCE) was still very young and his stepmother, Queen Tawosret, became regent. She was left in sole possession of the throne when the young king, a weak and sickly youth whose mummified body has a distorted left leg attributed to polio, died barely six years later. Siptah was buried in the Valley of the Kings, but his tomb (KV47) was badly sited; due to the poor condition of the rock little of its decoration survives, although what does remain is of high quality. His small mortuary temple, located between the temples of Thutmose IV and Merneptah on the west bank of the Nile, was later taken over by his stepmother. His mummy was among those recovered in 1898 from the royal cache in KV35, the tomb of Amenhotep II.

Supported by her astute Syrian chancellor, Bay, Tawosret ruled Egypt in her own name for a further two years (c.1188–c.1186BCE). Little is known in detail of Bay's career, but he clearly wielded a great deal of power, and was buried in the Valley of the Kings. Paintings in his tomb (KV13) show the chancellor with funerary deities, a privilege normally reserved for kings. Perhaps under Bay's influence, Tawosret is believed to have instigated military campaigns in Sinai and Palestine, and her name appears on monuments at Abydos, Hermopolis, and Memphis. Aged around 65 at her death, she was buried in tomb KV14 in the Valley of the Kings, the tomb her husband Sety II had intended to share with her. The decoration comprises extracts from the *Book of the Dead* and scenes of Tawosret with funerary deities. Tawosret's body has not been identified, but her granite sarcophagus was reused for the burial of a 20th-Dynasty prince.

Little is known of the political events surrounding the transition of power from Tawosret, the last ruler of the 19th Dynasty, to Sethnakht (c.1186–c.1184BCE), the founder of the 20th Dynasty, except that Sethnakht appears to have had no immediate connection with the previous ruling family. He may, however, have been distantly related to it, possibly yet another descendant of Ramesses II. Sethnakht clearly

**OPPOSITE**
The deceased's journey through the underworld culminated in the encounter with its ruler Osiris, depicted here, on the wall of Queen Tawosret's tomb, seated on a throne and holding a crook and flail. Symbols of herding and agriculture, the crook and flail also represented the king's authority over his people, and as such were key items of royal regalia.

The northern wall of Queen
Tawosret's burial chamber of
KV14 is decorated with the
final scene of the *Book of
Caverns*. Above the ram-headed
solar deity, worshipers hail the
sun, which is represented by
a solar disc and a scarab, as
it is reborn at dawn.

**OPPOSITE**

Geb, the earth god, painted
on one of the pillars of the
sarcophagus hall of Queen
Tawosret. The wall behind
is adorned with scenes
from the *Book of Gates*.

regarded himself as the legitimate successor of Sety II, and may have established himself
as a rival ruler during the reign of Tawosret, Sety's widow. In the *Great Harris Papyrus*,
Sethnakht's son, Ramesses III, unequivocally asserts his father's legitimacy and divine
status: "When the gods thought to make peace, to establish the land in harmony, they
placed their son [Sethnakht], who came from their limbs, to be ruler of every land,
upon the great throne... he cleansed the great throne of Egypt."

Sethnakht inherited a nation whose economy was in decline, and whose
stability and morale had been weakened by a series of ineffectual rulers. He left no
significant monuments at Thebes, but the line he founded was to be the last great native
dynasty to rule Egypt. He died after just two years on the throne, and was buried in an
extension of Tawosret's tomb (KV14) in the Valley of the Kings. Rather than using her
burial chamber, he had a second pillared chamber created for his own sarcophagus. The
fate of his mummy is unclear; one of his coffins was found in the royal cache in KV35,
suggesting that his body, too, may at some point have been moved there.

# UNITED WITH ETERNITY
## RAMESSES III (c.1184–c.1153 BCE)

Sethnakht's son and successor, Ramesses III, was the last of Egypt's great warrior kings. However, at the time of his accession acceptance of the new dynasty was far from universal: an inscription on the pylon of his mortuary temple at Medinet Habu in western Thebes reminds his people that "I did not take my office by robbery, but the crown was set on my head willingly."

By the time Ramesses inherited the throne c.1184 BCE, Egypt was once more on the defensive against its enemies. The eastern Mediterranean world was in political confusion; for the past century, Ramesses II's peace treaty with the Hittites had cushioned Egypt from attack, but now the Hittite empire was crumbling, and Egypt itself was threatened by invasion. The invaders were the same Libyans and "Sea Peoples" who had proved so troublesome during the reign of Merneptah.

In the fifth year of his reign, Ramesses III led his armies on a victorious expedition against the Libyans, who had formed an alliance with the tribes of the Western Desert and were planning an attack on the Delta. Three years later, he engaged the Sea Peoples, who, having wreaked havoc in Syria and Palestine, launched a two-pronged attack on Egypt by land and sea. In response, Ramesses moved his troops into Palestine, while positioning the navy to meet the enemy fleet, as inscriptions in his mortuary temple record: "I organized my frontier in Djahay [in southern Palestine], it being prepared before them—the princes, garrison commanders, and warriors. I caused the Nile mouths to be prepared like a strong wall, with warships, galleys, and coasters."

While Ramesses was occupied in repulsing the Sea Peoples, the Libyans had quietly managed to settle a large part of the western Delta, and, encouraged by this success, their leader Meshesher launched another attack, this time a full-scale invasion of Egyptian territory. Ambushed by Ramesses' troops before they had even left the Delta, the Libyans surrendered.

After he had thus established Egypt's security, Ramesses presided over relative peace for the remainder of his reign, enabling him to build and endow temples

**OPPOSITE**
A relief from the third corridor of the tomb of Ramesses III showing the king wearing the Blue Crown (*khepresh*), also known as the War Crown. The pair of cobras on his brow wear the White Crown of Upper Egypt and the Red Crown of Lower Egypt, identifying them as the goddesses Nekhbet and Wadjet, who personified and protected the Nile Valley and the Delta. Curiously, the colours of the crowns have been reversed, perhaps in error.

at the great religious centers of Memphis and Heliopolis in the north, and at Thebes in the south. A record of Ramesses III's donations to religious foundations is contained in the *Great Harris Papyrus*, compiled at the close of his reign and the longest papyrus in existence.

Ramesses III died in the 31st year of his reign, shortly after the discovery of an assassination plot instigated by one of his wives, Tiy, who planned to replace her husband with her son. A contemporary papyrus, now in the Museo Egizio, Turin, Italy, records that the prince was forced to commit suicide, but the fate of Tiy and the other conspirators is unknown. There is no evidence that the king suffered any harm.

Ramesses III was buried in a tomb in the Valley of the Kings (KV11) that had originally been intended for his father. His mummy, which shows signs of arteriosclerosis, was among those found in DB320, the royal cache at Deir el-Bahri.

Throughout his reign, Ramesses III sought to emulate his predecessor Ramesses II, both on the battlefield and in the scale of his building projects. Like his famous namesake, he erected a number of monuments to the deities of Karnak, while at Luxor he initiated a program of decoration in the temple of Amun. His principal monument at Karnak was a vast barque shrine now situated in the first courtyard; at the time of building, this was the temple forecourt. Part of Ramesses III's dedication inscription reads: "I made [it] for you…in your city of Waset [Thebes], in front of your forecourt to the Lord of the Gods, being the temple of Ramesses [III] in the Estate of Amun, to remain as long as the heavens bear the sun. I built it, and sheathed it with sandstone, bringing great doors of fine gold, and I filled its treasuries with offerings that my hands had brought."

In effect a small temple, Ramesses III's shrine comprised an entrance pylon leading into a pillared court fronting a portico and a hypostyle hall; at the rear were three shrines for the sacred barques of Amun, Mut, and Khonsu (the Theban

**ABOVE**

To preserve symmetry in inscriptions, Egyptian hieroglyphs could be written from right to left or left to right. On this lintel in the mortuary temple of Ramesses III, a winged solar disc guards the king's royal names, written inside protective cartouches. Hieroglyphs flanking the central *ankh* sign identify Ramesses as "Son of Ra" and "The Good God."

**OPPOSITE**

Egyptian temples were originally decorated in bright colors, and Ramesses' mortuary temple is remarkable for the preservation of its painted reliefs. These columns in the second court flank the entrance to the temple's inner chambers, and are decorated with scenes of the king worshiping the fertility god Amun-Min and other deities.

triad). On the east and west of the courtyard, square pillars feature colossal figures of Ramesses in the form of the god Osiris; in the wall reliefs he is shown participating in temple festivals.

Ramesses III's most impressive monument, his memorial or mortuary temple, is located at Medinet Habu on the west bank of the Nile and called the "Mansion of Millions of Years of King Usermaatra Meryamun [Ramesses III], United with Eternity." The modern Arabic name can be translated as "Town of Habu," and may refer to the nearby temple of Amenhotep son of Hapu, architect and chief adviser to Amenhotep III. Known to the ancient Egyptians as Djeme, the site was believed to be sacred to the primeval gods of Egypt; a small temple had existed there from at least the time of Hatshepsut. This temple was incorporated within Ramesses III's grand scheme and enclosed within its massive fortified walls.

The temple's distinctive walls, built of mudbrick faced with stone, appear to have been modeled on Syrian fortifications; the gateway, too, has many defensive features, notably the sloping plinths at the base, which could keep attackers away from the walls while bringing them into range of the bowmen concealed high in the tower. In Ramesses III's time, however, the tower served a more peaceful purpose. Its upper apartments served as a kind of pleasure palace, where the king could sit and enjoy the breeze, looking out over the temple harbor to watch the coming and going of religious processions. Reliefs on the walls show Ramesses III relaxing with the ladies of his harem, and playing the board game *senet*.

Inside the gateway, the approach to Ramesses III's temple was through a beautiful garden with pools, trees, and flowerbeds. The king was an enthusiastic gardener—according to the *Great Harris Papyrus*, he planted a total of 541 gardens and vineyards at temples around Egypt during his reign.

The mortuary temple itself is conventional in plan—based on the Ramesseum, the temple of Ramesses II, built a century before. Laid out along a single axis, reflecting the processional nature of temple ritual, it comprises two pylons, two colonnaded courts, a portico, a hypostyle hall, and a vestibule surrounded by small chapels and storerooms.

To the south of the temple was a small palace complex, adjoining the first court and connected to it by a "Window of Appearances," a kind of balcony where Ramesses III would appear before the crowds assembled in the courtyard. The palace, used by the king when he came to Thebes for its great annual festivals, consisted of a large anteroom, a small audience hall with a raised alabaster dais for the king's throne, and at the back a suite of small private rooms, including a bedroom and bathroom. Like all royal residences, the palace was decorated with brightly colored wall paintings and glazed tiles. Miniature masterpieces in their own right, the tiles from this palace

**ABOVE**

Five colored glazed tiles from Ramesses III's palace at Medinet Habu, each depicting different peoples conquered by Ramesses III. From left to right: a Nubian, a Syrian, a Bedouin Shasu, and a Hittite.

**OPPOSITE**

A fortified doorway at Medinet Habu with a scene of Ramesses III's victory over the Sea Peoples' coalition formed from enemies of the pharaoh.

The primary role of the pharaoh was to ensure divine order, or *maat,* throughout the Egyptian state and the cosmos. In this scene from the tomb of Ramesses III, the king offers a seated figure of Maat, personified as a goddess, to the enthroned Osiris as a sign that he has fulfilled this obligation.

represent a favorite royal theme—bound foreign captives, symbolizing Ramesses' victory over enemy powers and thus the fulfillment of the king's divine duty to defend Egypt and maintain divine order.

The theme of Ramesses III as the defender of Egypt continues in the decoration of the temple's exterior. On the pylon Ramesses is shown in the traditional "smiting" attitude of the warrior king, with one hand seizing foreign enemies by the hair and the other raised and wielding a mace, with which he is about to deal them a lethal blow (see page 180). To either side of the doorway, stelae extol his triumph over invaders and exhort the loyalty of the populace.

The rear of the northern tower is carved with scenes from Ramesses III's first campaign against the Libyans, a theme that continues along the temple's northern and western walls, where he is seen battling the Sea Peoples. An account of the second Libyan campaign is found inside the first court, where scribes are shown enumerating the enemy's losses. Ramesses' campaigns did much to enrich Egypt, since the invading groups were not armies as such, but whole tribes of settlers, including women, children, and herds. The captives were enslaved—some as laborers, some as warriors for the Egyptian army—and their possessions were seized for the royal treasury.

The remainder of the interior decoration is devoted to the religious function of the temple. In the second court, the scenes focus on the festivals of the necropolis god Sokar (see illustration on page 71) and the fertility god Amun-Min. The temple sanctuary was, as usual, dedicated to Amun during the king's lifetime (see pages 148–150), and in keeping with the funerary nature of the temple, small suites of chapels were dedicated to Osiris and the solar god Ra-Harakhty.

On the southern exterior wall of the temple, a vast and detailed temple calendar gives details of all the festivals celebrated at Medinet Habu, together with the offerings made at each. The normal daily offerings consisted of 3,220 loaves of bread, 24 cakes, 144 jugs of beer, 32 geese, and several jars of wine; at each new moon, these

were supplemented by an extra 356 loaves, 14 cakes, 34 jugs of beer, an ox, 16 birds, and 23 jars of wine. Once these had been offered to the gods and goddesses of the temple, they were distributed among the priests as payment for their services.

Ramesses III was buried in the Valley of the Kings in a tomb (KV11) originally intended for his father Sethnakht. However, soon after construction had begun, the excavators had run into the tomb of Amenmesse (KV10) and abandoned work. Ramesses' tomb builders resumed excavations, solving the problem by shifting the axis of the tomb to the right.

Open since antiquity, the tomb is often called "Bruce's Tomb" after the Scottish traveler James Bruce, who visited Thebes in 1786 and later returned to make copies of the paintings. It has several novel features, including a second antechamber and a series of small painted chambers on either side of the second corridor. Decorated with images of jars, weapons, and other objects, these may have been intended for the storage of grave goods. The religious decoration consists chiefly of extracts from the *Book of Gates* and a new funerary text, the *Book of the Earth*, which presents yet another vision of the sun god's journey through the night. In this version, the reborn sun disc is raised from the earth by the god Nun, the embodiment of the primordial waters of creation.

In addition to his own funerary monuments, Ramesses prepared opulent tombs for the members of his family. At least five of his sons were buried in the Valley of the Queens—Pareherwenemef (QV42), Sethherkhepeshef (QV43), Khaemwaset (QV44), Ramesses (QV53), and Amenherkhepeshef (QV55)—and others may have been buried in the Valley of the Kings in tombs KV3 and KV13.

The tombs of the princes are simple in design, consisting of a long, straight corridor ending in a burial chamber. The majority of the paintings show the princes as children, wearing the distinctive sidelock indicating youth, being presented to the gods and goddesses of the dead by their father. Elsewhere in the tombs, religious texts such as the *Book of Gates* and the *Book of the Dead* are illustrated.

A painting from a side room off the second corridor in the the tomb of Ramesses III showing Nile gods and goddesses representing the Egyptian provinces and bearing offerings of produce from the land and river. The figure on the left personifies the city of Heliopolis in the Nile Delta.

# DECLINE OF A ROYAL CITY
## RAMESSES IV TO RAMESSES XI (c.1153–c.1069 BCE)

Following the death of Ramesses III, Egypt's fortunes went into decline as a series of eight kings—all named Ramesses—occupied the throne in relatively quick succession. The fact that no single king reigned long enough to implement any long-term policy led to a weakening of central power and the absence of a solid foreign policy.

The decline in central royal authority led to an increase in the political power of Thebes in this period. With the court in the far-off Delta, the government of southern Egypt increasingly came under the control of the Theban priesthood of Amun and the priests' associates in the local administration, leading to the emergence of a priestly "dynasty" cemented by strategic intermarriages. The status attained by Amenhotep, High Priest of Amun under several of the later kings of the 20th Dynasty, was such that he felt sufficiently confident to have himself represented on the same scale as the king in temple reliefs at Karnak.

Another inevitable consequence of the lack of a powerful central authority was that Egypt's trade and revenue system suffered, and the economy began to crumble. At Thebes, interruptions in the supply of resources to state employees led to strikes, and eventually to a series of tomb-robbing scandals at the end of the dynasty. Similar scandals centered around the pilfering of state property from temple stores. Eventually this type of corruption permeated Thebes to such an extent that a large number of the population was implicated.

These circumstances led to a breakdown in social order, with high levels of crime and widespread civil unrest. To compound the situation, the Libyans who had caused such trouble for Ramesses III were now settling unchecked in the oases of the Western Desert, and gangs of bandits roamed the desert fringes, raiding unprotected settlements. By the end of the dynasty, the inhabitants of the isolated tombworkers' village at Deir el-Medina in western Thebes had been forced to abandon their village and take up residence inside the fortified walls of Ramesses III's temple at Medinet Habu.

**OPPOSITE**
A painting in the tomb of Ramesses VI showing the king worshiping the baboons who guard the Lakes of Fire in the Underworld. In Chapter 126 of the *Book of the Dead* the deceased prays to the baboons to purify him so that he may pass safely into the afterlife.

Although royal building continued at Thebes, it was on a greatly reduced scale, and the chief monuments to the later kings of the 20th Dynasty are their tombs in the Valley of the Kings. At Karnak, work continued on the rebuilding of the temple of Khonsu, which had been initiated under Ramesses III. Few 20th Dynasty rulers erected mortuary temples, although Ramesses IV (c.1153–c.1147BCE) built two small temples on the west bank, using stone taken from other temples in the area.

By the time of Ramesses VI (c.1143–c.1136BCE), the ruling house was in disarray, as members of the family fought for power among themselves. In an attempt to curb the power of the priests of Amun, Ramesses IX (c.1126–c.1108BCE) appointed his own sons to the Theban priesthood, and arranged marriages between his daughters and local nobles, but the days of his dynasty were numbered. Under his successor Ramesses X (c.1108–c.1099BCE), Egypt lost control of Nubia.

After these seven short-lived kings came the relatively long reign of Ramesses XI (c.1099–c.1069BCE), the last ruler of the 20th Dynasty. However, he was unable to reassert royal power in the south. The economy foundered, leading to famine and civil war, and by the end of his reign Thebes had come under the control of Libyan chieftains who assumed the title of High Priest of Amun for themselves.

It is likely that all the kings of the late 20th Dynasty were buried in the Valley of the Kings, although the tomb of Ramesses VIII (c.1129–c.1126BCE) has yet to be identified. The royal tombs are similar in plan, consisting of a long straight corridor ending in a burial chamber. A rare papyrus in the Museo Egizio in Turin shows the plan of the tomb of Ramesses IV (KV2); it includes the ancient names for the different parts of the tomb, shedding light on their function and religious significance. The entrance and the first two corridors are missing, but the third is designated the "fourth passage of the god," underlining the tomb's role in effecting the deceased and deified king's journey into the afterlife. The well room, which in this tomb substitutes for the antechamber, is called the "hall of waiting," and the burial chamber the "house of gold

wherein one rests." The designation of the rooms beyond the burial chamber—the "passageway of the god which is the *shabti*-place," "the resting place of the gods," the "treasury of perfection," and the "left-hand treasury,"—reflects their function as storage places for the king's burial goods and funerary equipment.

In general, the burial chambers were furnished with a stone sarcophagus to receive the royal mummy. However, KV1, the tomb of Ramesses VII (*c.*1136–*c.*1129BCE), which was clearly prepared in haste, simply has a depression cut into the floor, which was covered with an improvised lid fashioned from the base of a sarcophagus.

The decoration in the tombs is mainly of scenes from the traditional royal funerary texts: the *Amduat*, the *Litany of Ra*, the *Book of Gates*, the *Book of Caverns*, the *Book of the Earth*, and the *Book of the Dead*. From the time of Ramesses IV an additional text appears on the tomb ceiling—the *Book of the Heavens*. Illustrating the passage of the

**RIGHT**
Two golden figures of the sky goddess Nut stretch the entire length of the ceiling in the burial chamber of Ramesses VI. The figure on the right represents the night sky when the sun god, having been swallowed at sunset, travels through the body of the goddess to be reborn at dawn. The figure on the left represents the daytime sky, when Nut conceals the stars within her. On the wall below, the arms of the primordial deity Nun raise the newborn sun over the eastern horizon. The north wall has the first appearance of scenes from the *Book of Earth*.

190

A detail of the astronomical ceiling in the third corridor of the tomb of Ramesses IX showing the sun god's journey through the heavens. On the left a large serpent encloses the king's cartouche in its protective coils.

sun through the sky, it was a development of the astronomical ceilings found in earlier royal burial chambers. Despite the troubled era in which they were made, the tombs contain some fine decoration, most notably in KV19, the tomb of a son of Ramesses IX.

Few of the kings buried in these tombs were destined to rest in peace, due to an epidemic of tomb robberies during the reign of Ramesses IX. Practically everyone in the Theban administration was implicated, and after a series of local cover-ups, the king's vizier was dispatched to investigate in person. A fascinating account of his investigations can be found in the Abbot Papyrus in the British Museum.

Very often it transpired that the tomb robbers were the same men who had built the tombs, since they knew their layout and contents precisely. However, the removal and disposal of the stolen goods required accomplices, including local officials who were bribed to turn a blind eye. A favorite technique was to tunnel into a tomb from the back, leaving the sealed front entrance intact and the tomb apparently undisturbed. The robbers then worked at their leisure, taking the spoils to an obliging metalworker to be melted down before they were sold and the profits divided.

**ABOVE**
A scene from the *Book of Earth* in the burial tomb of Ramesses IX. It shows the reborn sun, supported by a scarab, flanked by the ram-headed Atum, god of the setting sun, and the scarab-headed Khepri, god of the rising sun.

At first, the tomb robbers concentrated on the long-forgotten tombs of the 17th Dynasty, but then, rather rashly, they moved on to more recent—and better guarded—burials, and ultimately to their own downfall. Under torture, they confessed to their activities, and the Abbott Papyrus records some of these confessions, which give a vivid account of the robbers' activities: "We opened their outer coffins, and their inner coffins in which they lay. We found the noble mummy of this king equipped with a sword. A large number of amulets and ornaments of gold were upon his neck, his mask of gold was upon him—the noble mummy of the king was completely covered with gold. His coffins were adorned with gold and silver inside and out, and inlaid with all kinds of precious stones. We collected the gold which we found on the noble mummy of this god, and on his amulets and jewels which were upon his neck, and on the coffins in which he lay."

Some of those arrested were exonerated—probably because at least one of the judges was involved in the robberies—but those convicted were executed, since the violation of a royal tomb constituted blasphemy as well as robbery.

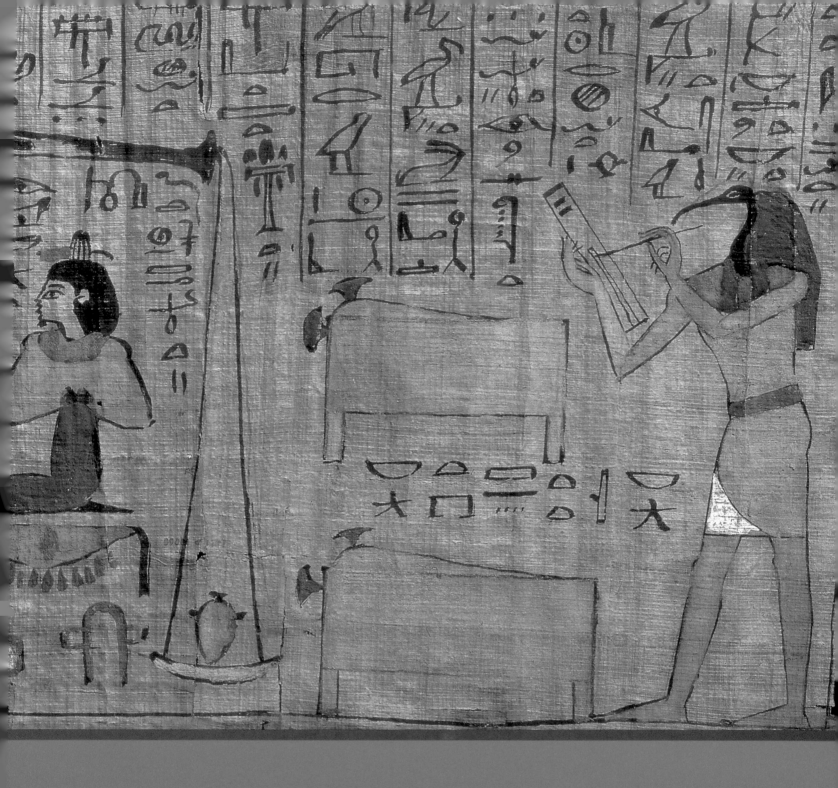

# EPILOGUE

## AFTER THE NEW KINGDOM (c.1069bce–c.641ce)

# DISUNITY AND FOREIGN RULE
## 3RD INTERMEDIATE PERIOD
## (C.1069BCE–C.747BCE)

**OPPOSITE**
Probably the daughter of the High Priest Pinudjem I, Maakara was the first of a dynasty of priestesses known as the Divine Wives of Amun. Her colorful and richly gilded exterior coffin was found in the royal cache at Deir el-Bahri.

**BELOW**
These opulent gold bracelets from Pinudjem II's mummy testify to the near-royal status of the High Priests of Amun at Thebes in the 21st Dynasty.

At the end of the 20th Dynasty, Egypt was controlled by three men. Ramesses XI (c.1099–c.1069BCE) was still nominally ruler of the whole country, but his power effectively extended only to the Memphis region and Middle Egypt. Southern Egypt and Nubia was governed from Thebes by Herihor (c.1080–c.1070BCE), the Libyan-descended High Priest of Amun, while much of the Nile Delta was controlled from Tanis by another Libyan, Smendes, who may have been Herihor's son.

Following the deaths of Ramesses XI and Herihor, Smendes (c.1069–c.1043BCE) assumed the role of sole ruler of Egypt, and thus became the first king of the 21st Dynasty. In reality, however, there continued to be two royal houses, one based at Tanis and the other at Thebes. Egyptologists refer to this era as the 3rd Intermediate Period (c.1069–c.747BCE), though in contrast to former times of national disunity these families generally maintained friendly relations with one another, further cemented by intermarriage.

By this time important changes had occurred in Egypt's economy and foreign relations. Most of Egypt's land was now in private ownership—though it was still subject to taxation—and the decline of royal power in recent decades had severely diminished Egypt's role in Near Eastern affairs. The relative poverty of the royal treasury may have played a part in the transfer of power c.945BCE to another Libyan family, the 22nd Dynasty, which was originally from the Delta city of Bubastis but ruled, like its predecessors, from Tanis.

In an attempt to assert control over the whole of Egypt, the new dynasty abolished the hereditary offices of Theban officials and installed their own sons as high priests. Predictably, these initiatives were met first with resistance and then with open revolt. In response, the 22nd-Dynasty kings created an official co-dynasty, which later became known as the 23rd Dynasty (c.818–c.715BCE), to reestablish control over southern Egypt.

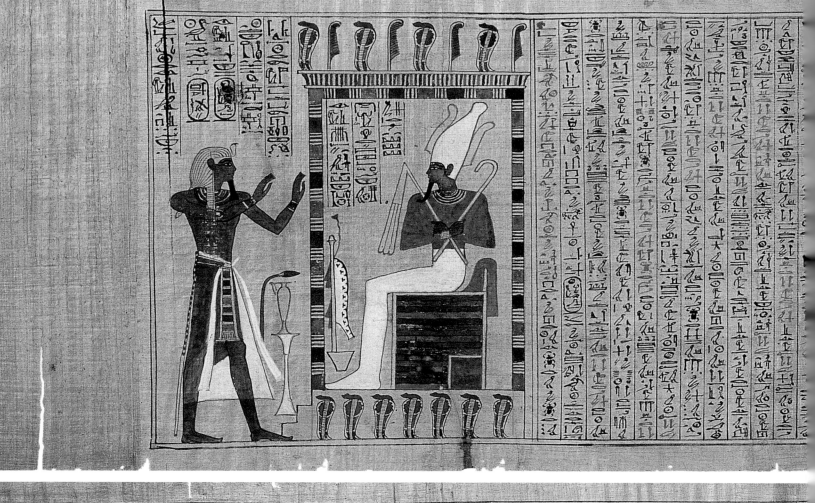

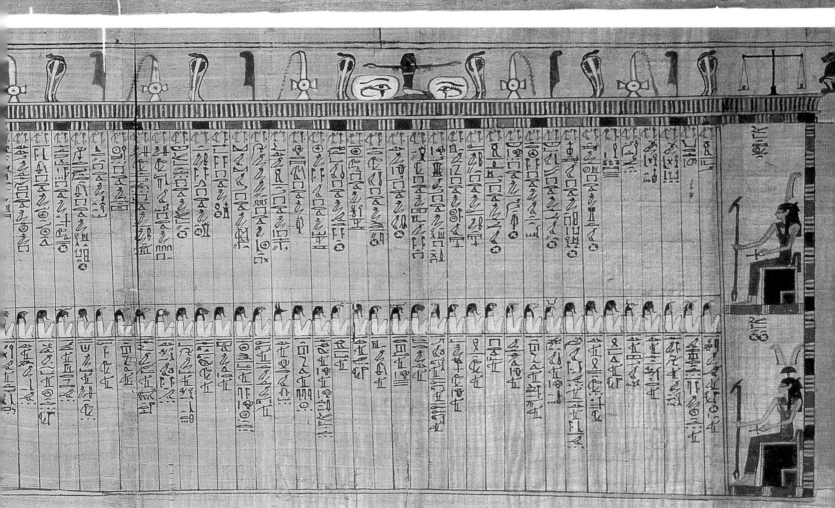

There was little royal building at Thebes during this period, since royal burials now took place at Tanis, but the high priests continued to erect monuments to Amun. At Karnak, Herihor had enlarged the temple of Khonsu, adding a courtyard and a pillared hall, where he is shown on the same scale as Ramesses XI. Furthermore, Herihor's name is written inside a royal cartouche, suggesting that he viewed himself as the king's coregent. Work at the Khonsu temple continued under Herihor's successor as high priest, Pinudjem I, who also usurped a number of Ramesses II's monuments. The high priests of the 22nd and 23rd Dynasties planned to enclose the courtyard in front of the temple of Amun, but only the colonnades were completed.

Perhaps as a result of the recent tomb-robbing scandals (see page 192), the Theban elite of this period preferred to be buried in unmarked pits or shafts, ending the long tradition of decorated tomb chapels and large assemblages of burial goods. However, the coffins in which they were buried were very elaborate. Decorated with funerary texts and paintings of protective deities, such coffins may have taken over some of the earlier functions of the tomb chapel.

For the kings of the 22nd Dynasty, Near Eastern affairs were a pressing issue. The Assyrians, a warlike people of northeastern Mesopotamia, were embarking on a period of imperial expansion, but the Egyptians were more concerned with events in Palestine. In *c.*925BCE Sheshonq I (*c.*945–*c.*924BCE)—the biblical Shishak—sacked Jerusalem and captured Judah; this reassertion of Egyptian influence in Palestine is commemorated in Sheshonq I's victory reliefs at Karnak.

Within Egypt, local factions continued to increase in power as rival branches of the royal family intermarried, creating complex and conflicting systems of loyalty. Inevitably, this led to the emergence of rival claimants to the throne. In *c.*818BCE, Pedubastis I (*c.*818–*c.*793BCE) declared himself king, marking the start proper of the 23rd Dynasty. By the end of the dynasty, there were a number of branches of the royal family ruling simultaneously from centers in the Nile Delta and the northern Nile Valley.

**PREVIOUS PAGES**
The *Book of the Dead* of
Pinudjem I. During the 3rd
Intermediate Period, the High
Priests of Amun assumed royal
dress and titles, hence the
hieroglyphs on Pinudjem's
funerary papyrus that identify
him as "King of Upper Egypt."

**LEFT**
The colors are excellently
preserved on this painted
wooden votive stela, *c*.900BCE,
dedicated by the noblewoman
Djedamuniuankh, who
appears on the right. The
bottom register depicts tombs
in the Theban necropolis.

**OPPOSITE**
A Theban 22nd-Dynasty
bronze figurine, inlaid with
gold, silver and electrum, that
represents the Divine Wife of
Amun Karomama. Her dress
is in the form of wings that
envelop her hips; the hands
would once have held rattles.

At the same time, another Delta family from Sais (the 24th Dynasty) gained control of the western Delta, and began to extend its territory southward.

Egypt was now in chaos, its eastern borders under threat from the Assyrians, while in the south a powerful Kushite (Nubian) kingdom was expanding northward from Napata through the Nile Valley toward the Delta. The Nubian Piy (*c*.747–*c*.716BCE) commemorated his victories over the northern forces on stelae at Memphis and Karnak, but seems not to have consolidated his gains. By *c*.716BCE the Napatan king Shabaqo (*c*.716–*c*.702BCE), Piy's brother, had completed the conquest of Egypt, establishing the 25th Dynasty.

# THE LAST EGYPTIAN PHARAOHS
## THE LATE PERIOD (c.747BCE–332BCE)

Known as the Late Period, the four centuries from the 25th to the 30th Dynasties (c.747–343BCE) were characterized by periods of foreign control interspersed with the rule of Egypt's last indigenous rulers.

In his attempt to restore stability to Egypt, Shabaqo established his capital at Memphis and set about creating a kingship consciously modeled on that of the Old Kingdom. Shabaqo's reverence for the past set the tone for the later rulers of the dynasty, who vied to surpass one another in showing concern for Egyptian religion and traditions, adopting traditional dress and erecting monuments based on Old Kingdom prototypes. Under Shabaqo's successor, Taharqo (690–664BCE), a magnificent kiosk was erected in front of the temple of Amun at Karnak. Taharqo also commissioned a large ritual structure beside the temple's sacred lake, and added a colonnade to the temple of Montu.

It was during the reign of Taharqo that the inevitable Assyrian attacks on Egypt began. In 669BCE Assyria conquered Egypt and installed a Saite family, the 26th Dynasty, as vassal rulers to protect Assyrian territories in Syria and Palestine from the 25th Dynasty, who had withdrawn to its Nubian heartland. Assyrian military officials based in Egypt were responsible for Egypt's foreign affairs and taxation, and the Saite kings were obliged to pay tribute to their masters in the way that Near Eastern states had once paid tribute to Egypt.

However, the Assyrian's expansion into Egypt had overstretched their vast empire, and within a few years the 26th Dynasty began to assert its independence, establishing its capital at Memphis. Like the previous dynasty, it exploited ancient tradition to

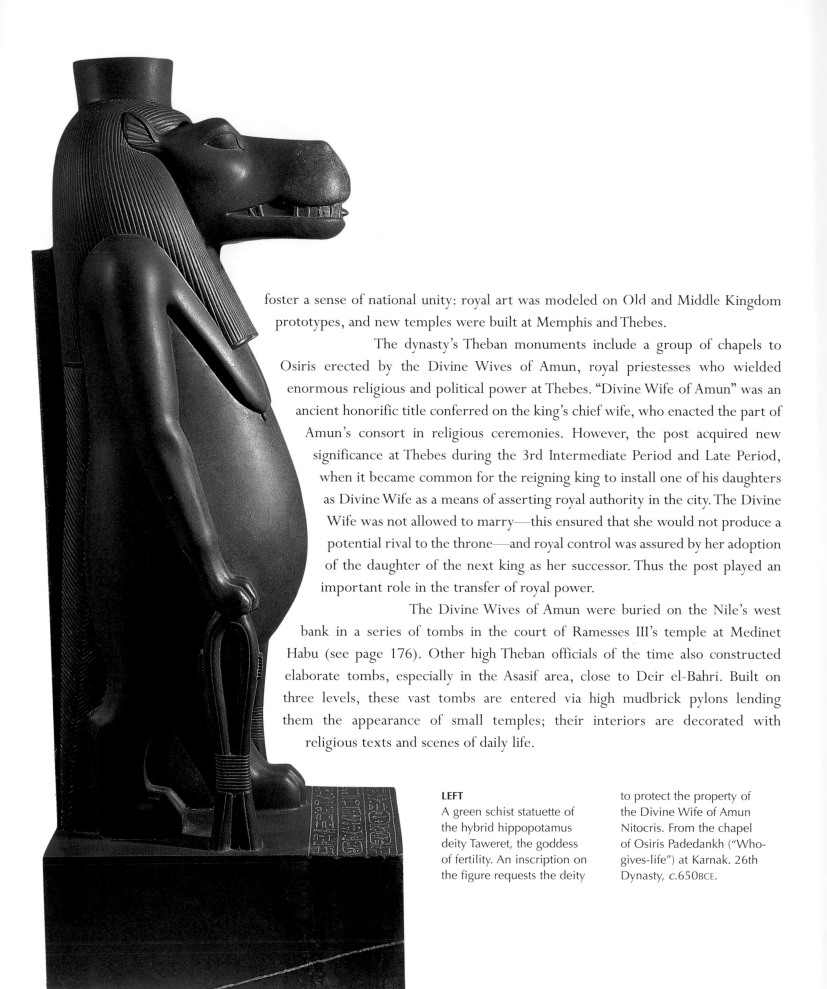

foster a sense of national unity: royal art was modeled on Old and Middle Kingdom prototypes, and new temples were built at Memphis and Thebes.

The dynasty's Theban monuments include a group of chapels to Osiris erected by the Divine Wives of Amun, royal priestesses who wielded enormous religious and political power at Thebes. "Divine Wife of Amun" was an ancient honorific title conferred on the king's chief wife, who enacted the part of Amun's consort in religious ceremonies. However, the post acquired new significance at Thebes during the 3rd Intermediate Period and Late Period, when it became common for the reigning king to install one of his daughters as Divine Wife as a means of asserting royal authority in the city. The Divine Wife was not allowed to marry—this ensured that she would not produce a potential rival to the throne—and royal control was assured by her adoption of the daughter of the next king as her successor. Thus the post played an important role in the transfer of royal power.

The Divine Wives of Amun were buried on the Nile's west bank in a series of tombs in the court of Ramesses III's temple at Medinet Habu (see page 176). Other high Theban officials of the time also constructed elaborate tombs, especially in the Asasif area, close to Deir el-Bahri. Built on three levels, these vast tombs are entered via high mudbrick pylons lending them the appearance of small temples; their interiors are decorated with religious texts and scenes of daily life.

**LEFT**
A green schist statuette of the hybrid hippopotamus deity Taweret, the goddess of fertility. An inscription on the figure requests the deity to protect the property of the Divine Wife of Amun Nitocris. From the chapel of Osiris Padedankh ("Who-gives-life") at Karnak. 26th Dynasty, c.650BCE.

**ABOVE**
A relief from the tomb at
el-Asasif of Montumenhat,
a 25th-Dynasty mayor of
Thebes, showing a seated
woman eating figs while
holding a child.

Egypt in this period was increasingly being drawn into the Mediterranean world. The Egyptian army was already dependent upon Greek mercenaries, and the economy was increasingly reliant on Mediterranean trade. From the 26th Dynasty, Greek merchants were allowed to establish trading centers in the Nile Delta, and settlement was encouraged. This friendly policy towards the Greeks eventually drew Egypt into the conflict between Greece and the new rising power of the region: Persia.

At the height of its authority, the Persian empire extended from Libya to the Indus. It was divided into around 20 provinces, or satrapies, each contributing tax and tribute to the Persian king. In the spring of 525BCE the Persians, led by Cambyses, defeated the Egyptian army at Pelusium in the Delta and Egypt became a satrapy of Persia. For the first time in its history the country was ruled directly by a foreign power, whose kings are referred to as comprising the 27th Dynasty (525–404BCE).

Recognizing the key role that temples played in the government of Egypt, the Persians consolidated their hold over the country by cultivating the support of the priesthood. There are few traces of the Persian period at Thebes: the Persians tried to act the part of pharaohs, but their rule was unpopular. There were numerous revolts inspired by Greek victories over their mutual enemy, and the invaders were finally expelled in 404BCE by Amyrtaios of Sais, the only king of the 28th Dynasty. In 399BCE he was deposed by Nepherites I, from the Delta city of Mendes. Nepherites and his successors (the 29th Dynasty, 399–380BCE) kept the Persians at bay before they were displaced by the 30th Dynasty (380–343BCE)—the last indigenous Egyptian rulers.

The 30th Dynasty were strongly nationalistic, especially in their devotion to traditional cults. They added buildings to many of Egypt's major shrines, including the temple of Amun at Karnak, where Nectanebo I (380–362BCE) erected the massive 1st Pylon. But they too had to contend with constant attempts by the Persians to reconquer Egypt. Eventually, Nectanebo II (360–343BCE)—the last native pharaoh—was defeated by Artaxerxes III, marking the beginning of the Second Persian Period, or 31st Dynasty (343–332BCE).

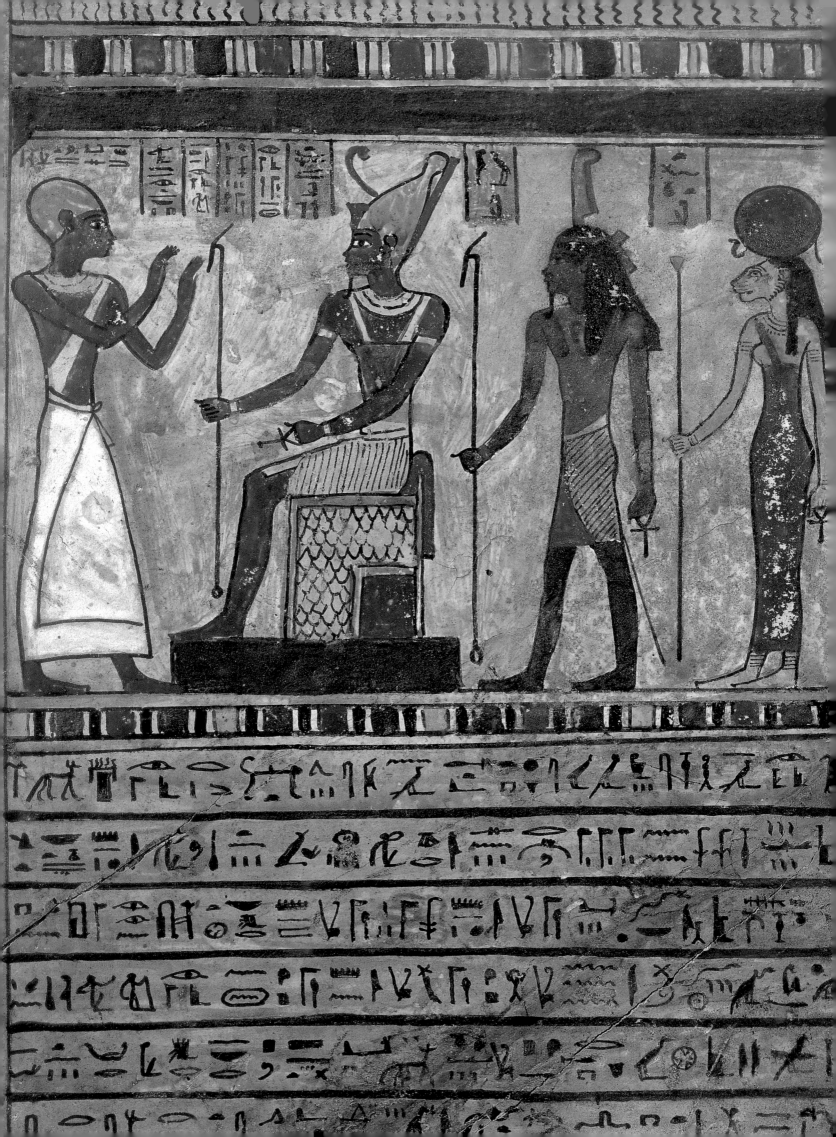

# GREEKS AND ROMANS
## PTOLEMAIC TO BYZANTINE PERIODS (332BCE–641CE)

In 332BCE the second Persian occupation of Egypt ended with the arrival of the armies of Alexander the Great. Born in Macedonia in 352BCE, Alexander was the son of Philip II of Macedon, though a later Egyptian story claimed that he was really the secret son of Nectanebo II, the last indigenous king of Egypt. The Persians had been unpopular rulers, while the Greeks were longstanding allies; from this point of view, Alexander's conquest of Egypt brought a sense of renewal rather than invasion. Alexander was greatly attracted to Egyptian culture and established a new capital at Alexandria in the Nile Delta, which he planned to make the capital of his empire.

However, Alexander died in Babylon just nine years later while on campaign, and the government of Egypt eventually passed to his friend and general Ptolemy, who established a new ruling dynasty. Reigning as Ptolemy I (305–285BCE), he was careful to uphold the traditional role of the pharaoh as the dutiful servant of the gods, encouraging the study of ancient Egyptian history and religion; during his reign the priest Manetho of Sebennytos began compiling his great history of the kings of Egypt, the *Aegyptiaca*, which became the chief source for later historians.

While the Ptolemies ruled from Alexandria, they were careful to cultivate the support of the temple priesthoods, especially in southern Egypt, where an ambitious program of temple building was initiated. At Luxor temple, Alexander—who styled himself the Son of Amun—had dedicated a new barque shrine for Amun within the god's sanctuary, while at Karnak a new sanctuary had been constructed in the name of Philip Arrhidaeus (323–317BCE), his halfbrother and shortlived heir.

Following their example, a series of Ptolemaic rulers added a number of features to the Karnak complex, extending the temples of Ptah, Montu, and Khonsu. Beside the temple of Khonsu, a new temple was erected, dedicated to Opet, the goddess of motherhood. On the west bank of the Nile, the Ptolemies extended the small temple of Amun at Medinet Habu, while at Deir el-Medina a new temple to Hathor was constructed on the site of the ancient foundation. At Deir el-Bahri,

Ptolemy VIII (170–116BCE) created a small shrine to the deified Egyptian sages Imhotep and Amenhotep son of Hapu.

Notwithstanding all their efforts, the Ptolemies were not universally popular; under their rule, Greek became the official language and the Greek-speaking classes enjoyed superior status, while the indigenous Egyptians were relegated to second-class citizens and taxed heavily. There were revolts against their rule at Thebes on several occasions, most notably during the reign of Ptolemy V (205–180BCE).

Despite the Ptolemies' efforts to restore Egypt's former glory, they were powerless to resist the rise of a new Mediterranean power—Rome. Despite the efforts of Queen Cleopatra VII (51–30BCE), who formed an alliance with Julius Caesar and later the Roman general Mark Antony (Marcus Antonius) in an audacious bid to establish a new Egyptian empire in the eastern Mediterranean, the forces of Ptolemaic resistance were conclusively defeated at the naval battle of Actium in 31BCE. The following year Octavian—the future emperor Augustus—captured Alexandria, both Cleopatra and Caesar's son died, and Egypt became a province of the Roman empire.

**ABOVE**
A Ptolemaic temple frieze showing part of a procession of Nile gods and goddesses bearing the produce of Egypt, to represent the bounty provided by the fertile river.

**OPPOSITE**
The ceremonial gateway in front of the temple of Khonsu at Karnak, erected in the reign of Ptolemy III (246–221BCE).

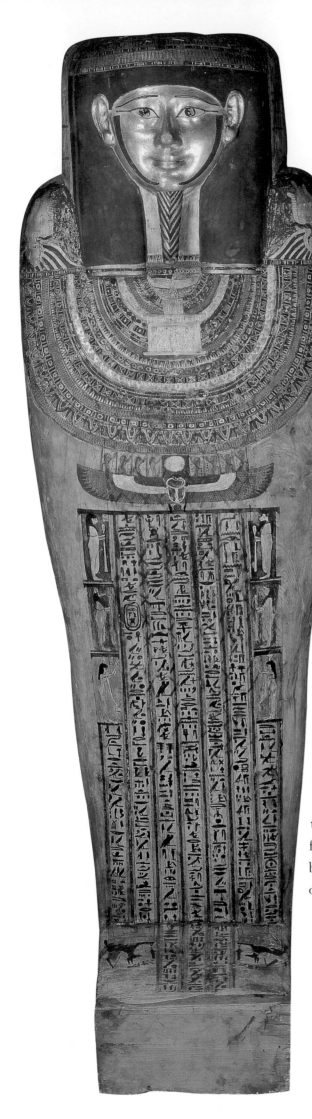

The Romans were principally interested in Egypt as a supplier of grain to their growing empire. Since the temple administrators played a key role in the collection of grain and taxation revenues, it was in the emperors' interest to cultivate their support by maintaining the royal custom of building and endowing temples. At Thebes, however, their contributions were modest, consisting of minor additions to temples at Karnak and Medinet Habu.

While it was far from the center of power in this period, Thebes remained famous and became a burgeoning center of tourism, attracting Greek and Roman visitors to its ancient sites. Two of the principal attractions were the Ramesseum and the tombs in the Valley of the Kings, where more than 2,000 examples of classical graffiti attest to visits spanning a period of 800 years from the 3rd century BCE to the 6th century CE. The chief attractions, though, were the two huge seated statues of Amenhotep III known as the Colossi of Memnon (see page 90). Emperors Hadrian (117–138CE) and Septimius Severus (193–211CE) were among those who visited the Colossi to hear the northern statue "sing" at dawn, a phenomenon probably arising from the expansion, as the stone warmed up, of cracks caused by earthquakes. After repairs ordered by Severus, the "singing" ceased.

Few rock-cut tombs were built in Thebes after the Late Period, although some cemeteries contain small mudbrick tombs dating from Ptolemaic and Roman times. The majority of burials were in reused tombs and mass graveyards; one group of three New Kingdom tombs was found to contain almost 300 mummies of later periods. A few elite family burials have been found—again in reused tombs—from this time, with many of the bodies encased in elaborate, often very large, nesting coffins.

**OPPOSITE**
The gilded wooden inner coffin of Hornedjitef, High Priest of Amun and a high-ranking dignitary in the reign of Ptolemy III, 3rd century BCE. The mask offers an idealized, eternally young image of the deceased, with the golden skin of a divine being.

**RIGHT**
Although they were modeled on Egyptian prototypes, Ptolemaic royal statues often display a marked classical influence in the representation of facial features and hairstyles. This basalt figure may represent Caesarion, the son of Cleopatra VII and Julius Caesar.

During the 1st century CE, the new religion of Christianity began to filter into Egypt, and the caves and hills around Thebes became home to ascetic hermits and monastic communities. Monks took up residence in several of the royal tombs, while KV3, the tomb of a son of Ramesses III, was converted into a chapel. While many of the emperors were tolerant of Christians, there were episodes of persecution, especially in 303CE under Diocletian (284–305CE). It was around this time that revolts against the Romans became more common at Thebes, and a Roman military camp was established incorporating Luxor temple, which had fallen into disuse. A hall of Amenhotep III was modified to create a chapel for the cult of the emperor, and a small temple to the hybrid Greco-Egyptian god Serapis was built inside the enclosure wall.

Following the division of the Roman empire in 395CE, Egypt was ruled from Constantinople (Byzantium), the capital of the eastern empire. By the end of the 4th century Christianity had become the empire's official religion, and paganism was formally banned. In Egypt many ancient temples were destroyed by zealous Christians, but others owe their survival to their reuse as churches or monasteries: in the 6th century CE a church was built in Ramesses II's court in Luxor temple.

In 641CE, the Byzantine rulers of Egypt were forced out by the invading armies of the Caliph Omar, and Egypt became a part of the Arab empire, with a new capital near modern Cairo. The status of Thebes had been in decline since the capital had returned to the north in the late New Kingdom, and after nearly 30 centuries of prominence the city reverted to being a rural backwater. Over the following decades most of the inhabitants of Thebes adopted Islam, leading to a decline in the Christian community, and by the end of the 8th century CE there was only one active monastery in the area. In medieval times a local Islamic saint, Abu el-Haggag, was buried in a shrine on top of Luxor temple, which had become filled with debris. The mosque enclosing his shrine is still in use, continuing a 4,000-year tradition of worship at the site and linking modern citizens with their ancient ancestors.

**OPPOSITE, LEFT**
The painted interior of the lid from the coffin of Soter, archon (chief magistrate) of Thebes in the early 2nd century CE, from his family burial in a reused 19th-Dynasty tomb. The central figure is a Romanized representation of the Egyptian sky goddess Nut, surrounded by the signs of the zodiac, which had been newly introduced from Babylon.

**OPPOSITE, RIGHT**
In the Roman period, traditional mummy masks were replaced by funerary portraits. Dating from the 3rd century CE, this portrait of a Theban woman was painted on a plaster panel sewn to her linen mummy wrappings.

215

# GLOSSARY

**akh** A blessed, transfigured spirit resulting from the successful merging of the dead person's *ka* and *ba*.

**Amarna art** An artistic style developed during the reign of Akhenaten, who moved the court to el-Amarna. It is characterized by flowing lines and the exaggerated representation of physical features.

**ankh** "Life," better known by its hieroglyph, which constitutes a sacred emblem frequently employed as a decorative motif.

**Aten, the** The disc or orb of the sun, which came to be worshipped as a god.

**ba** The winged spirit of a dead person. Depicted with the body of a bird and head of the deceased, the *ba* was able to fly from the underworld to visit, unseen, the world of the living.

**barque** A divine boat in which deities were believed to travel. Models of sacred barques, carried on poles, were used for the transportation of the divine images kept in temples.

**Book of the Dead** A type of funerary text comprising a collection of magic spells, usually inscribed on papyrus, placed in the tomb to ensure the safe passage of the deceased in the afterlife. It succeeded the earlier Pyramid Texts and Coffin Texts.

**cache/cachette** A collection of objects deliberately hidden in antiquity. Examples include statues buried in temple courtyards and the groups of royal mummies reburied in new locations.

**canopic jars** A set of containers, usually pottery or stone, for the viscera of the deceased.

**cartonnage** A material comprised of layers of linen or papyrus soaked in plaster. Easily moulded when wet, and strong and light when dry, it was used widely for funerary masks and body casings.

**cartouche** A protective oval ring surrounding the ruler's birth name and throne name. The cartouche is an elongated form of the *shen* hieroglyph, meaning "eternity."

**cataracts** The rapids or waterfalls that make a river impassable to traffic. The first Nile cataract, at modern-day Aswan, marked the southern boundary of ancient Egypt.

**cenotaph** A symbolic tomb or a mortuary cult site that does not contain the owner's body.

**Coffin Texts** The term used by Egyptologists to describe a type of funerary text popular in the Middle Kingdom. Inscribed or painted on coffins, the texts were drawn from more than 1,100 spells that in turn derived from the earlier Pyramid Texts.

**electrum** A natural or man-made gold-silver alloy.

**faience** A quartz-based ceramic glazed in bright colors, usually blue, and used to create decorative items such as tiles, jewelry, and figurines.

**hieroglyph** From the Greek "sacred carved letters," a picture or symbol representing an object, concept, or sound used for inscriptions in temples and tombs. A shorthand "hieratic" form was used for writing on papyrus.

**Hypostyle Hall** A multi-columned hall, usually in a temple.

**inundation** The annual, life-giving Nile flood.

**ka** The "vital force" or "spirit double" of a person or a god. The *ka* of a mortal was created at birth; when the body died, the *ka* remained in existence and (an Egyptian hoped) successfully entered the afterlife, where it was sustained by grave goods and the votive offerings of the living

**kiosk** A small, free-standing temple building, often used as a way-station during processions and usually containing a pedestal for a divine barque.

**mastaba** A tomb with a low, rectangular superstructure and an underground burial chamber, common for wealthy private burials from the Old Kingdom onward.

**menat** A beaded necklace with a heavy counterpoise in the form of the goddess Hathor. The *menat* was a symbol of the goddess and was used as a rattle during her sacred rites.

**New Kingdom** Arguably the greatest era of Egyptian civilization, the period covering the 18th to 20th dynasties of pharaohs.

**Pharaoh** The Greek rendition of the royal epithet *per-aa* ("Great House"), used originally for the court or royal residence but used to refer to the king from the New Kingdom onward.

**pylon** The monumental entrance or gateway to an Egyptian temple or palace.

**scarab** A dung beetle, symbolic of rebirth and renewal, and used to represent Khepri, the god of the rising sun.

**shabti** A small funerary figure placed in the tomb to serve the dead in the afterlife.

**sistrum (pl. sistra)** A sacred rattle associated with goddesses such as Hathor, and used to provide percussion during temple rituals.

**stela (pl. stelae)** An inscribed commemorative panel, usually of stone, either free-standing or an integral part of a tomb or temple.

**tamarisk** A small tree whose wood was used to make items such as funerary models and furniture.

**uraeus** A cobra deity associated with the protection of the king, the *uraeus* often appears on royal crowns and jewelry.

**vizier** The king's chief minister who was in overall control of government.

**wadi** A normally dry watercourse subject to occasional flooding during rainfall.

# BIBLIOGRAPHY

Baines, J. and Malek, J. *Atlas of Ancient Egypt*. Phaidon Press: Oxford, 1989.

Bierbrier, M.L. *The Tomb-builders of the Pharaohs*. British Museum Press: London, 1982.

Bowman, A.K. *Egypt after the Pharaohs*. British Museum Press: London, 1986.

Clayton, Peter A. *Chronicle of the Pharaohs*. Thames and Hudson: London, 1994.

Egyptian Antiquities Organization. *Official Catalogue: The Egyptian Museum, Cairo*. Verlag Philipp von Zabern: Mainz, 1987.

Egyptian Antiquities Organization. *The Luxor Museum of Ancient Egyptian Art Guidebook*. Egyptian Antiquities Organization: Cairo, 1978.

Faulkner, R.O. *The Ancient Egyptian Book of the Dead*. British Museum Press: London, 1985.

Fletcher, J. *Ancient Egypt: Life, Myth and Art*. Duncan Baird Publishers and Stewart, Tabori and Chang: London and New York, 1999.

Fletcher, J. *Egypt's Sun King. Amenhotep III: An Intimate Chronicle of Ancient Egypt's Most Glorious Pharaoh*. Duncan Baird Publishers and Oxford University Press: London and New York, 2000.

Fletcher, J. *The Egyptian Book of Living and Dying*. Duncan Baird Publishers and Thorsons: London and New York, 2002.

Grimal, N. *A History of Ancient Egypt*. (Translated by Ian Shaw.) Blackwell Publishers: Oxford, 1992.

Hart, G. *Egyptian Myths*. British Museum Press: London, 1990.

Kamil, J. Luxor: *A Guide to Ancient Thebes*. Longman: London, 1973.

Kemp, B.J. *Ancient Egypt: Anatomy of a Civilization*. Routledge: London, 1989.

Kitchen, K.A. *Pharaoh Triumphant: The Life and Times of Ramesses II*. Aris and Phillips Ltd.: Warminster, England, 1982.

Kitchen, K.A. *The Third Intermediate Period in Egypt*. Aris and Phillips Ltd.: Warminster, England 1995.

Lichtheim, M. (ed.) *Ancient Egyptian Literature: A Book of Readings: The Old and Middle Kingdoms*. University of California Press: Berkeley, 1975.

Lichtheim, M. (ed.) *Ancient Egyptian Literature: A Book of Readings: The New Kingdom*. University of California Press: Berkeley, 1973.

Lichtheim, M. (ed.) *Ancient Egyptian Literature: A Book of Readings: The Late Period*. University of California Press: Berkeley, 1980.

Manley, B. *The Penguin Historical Atlas of Ancient Egypt*. Penguin Books: London, 2000.

Manniche, L. *City of the Dead: Thebes in Egypt*. British Museum Press: London, 1987.

McDermott, B. *Decoding Egyptian Hieroglyphs*. Duncan Baird Publishers and Chronicle: London and San Francisco, 2001.

Murnane, W. *United with Eternity: A Concise Guide to the Monuments of Medinet Habu*. University of Chicago Press, American University in Cairo Press: Chicago and Cairo, 1980.

Pemberton, D. *Travellers' Architectural Guides: Ancient Egypt*. Viking Penguin and Chronicle: London and San Francisco, 1992.

Quirke, S. *Who were the Pharaohs?* British Museum Press: London, 1990.

Quirke, S. *Ancient Egyptian Religion*. British Museum Press: London, 1992.

Reeves, N. *The Complete Tutankhamun: The King, the Tomb, the Royal Treasure*. Thames and Hudson: London, 1990.

Reeves, N. and Wilkinson, R.H. *The Complete Valley of the Kings*. Thames and Hudson: London, 1996.

Reeves, N. *Ancient Egypt: The Great Discoveries*. Thames and Hudson: London, 2000.

Riefstahl, E. *Thebes in the Time of Amunhotep III*. University of Oklahoma Press: Norman, Oklahoma, 1964.

Robins, G. *The Art of Ancient Egypt*. British Museum Press, 1999.

Romer, J. *The Valley of the Kings*. Weidenfeld & Nicholson: London, 1981.

Romer, J. *Ancient Lives: The Story of the Pharaoh's Tombmakers*. Weidenfeld & Nicholson: London, 2003.

Schafer, B.E. (ed.) *Temples of Ancient Egypt*. I.B. Tauris: London, 1998.

Shaw, I. and Nicholson, P. *The British Museum Dictionary of Ancient Egypt*. British Museum Press: London, 1995.

Silverman, P. (ed.) Ancient Egypt. Duncan Baird Publishers and Oxford University Press: London and New York, 2003.

Smith, W. Stevenson. *The Art and Architecture of Ancient Egypt*. Pelican Books: Harmondsworth, England, 1981.

Strudwick, N. and Strudwick, H. *Thebes in Egypt: A Guide to the Tombs and Temples of Ancient Luxor*. British Museum Press and Cornell University Press: London and New York, 1999.

Weeks, Kent R. (ed.) *Valley of the Kings*. White Star: Vercelli, Italy, 2001.

Wilkinson, R.H. *The Complete Temples of Ancient Egypt*. Thames and Hudson: London, 2000.

# INDEX

**NOTES:** Page references in *italics* refer to illustrations or maps. As in the text, pharaohs are referred to by their family name rather than by their nomen/prenomen; for example, the third pharaoh of the 19th Dynasty is indexed as Ramesses II not Usermaatra. However, Dynasties are indexed under name rather then number: Nineteenth Dynasty instead of 19th Dynasty.

# ACKNOWLEDGMENTS AND PICTURE CREDITS

## ACKNOWLEDGMENTS

The author would like to express many thanks to all the team at Duncan Baird Publishers, especially Christopher Westhorp, Peter Bently and Alice Gillespie, for their invaluable help in preparing this book. Thanks are also due to my colleagues at the British Museum, and to my family and friends for their support and encouragement.

The Publishers would like to thank Dr Bridget McDermott for her help during the development of the project.

## Captions for illustrations on pages 1–4
**1. (Half-title page)** A painted low relief from the tomb of Horemheb depicting him making an offering of wine to the goddess Hathor.
**2. (Opposite the title page)** A gilt relief from Tutankhamun's golden throne showing a duck flying over papyrus.
**3. (Title page)** A scarab detail from a gold and silver pectoral belonging to Tutankhamun.
**4. (Contents)** A wall-painting from the tomb of Queen Nefertari showing Isis.

## Captions for chapter opener illustrations
**14–15.** Painted funerary stela of Amenemhet (center), his wife Iji and son, 11th Dynasty.
**44–45.** A wall-painting from Horemheb's tomb showing Hathor (center) receiving an offering.
**132–133.** A scene from the Book of the Earth in a wall-painting from the tomb of Ramesses IX.
**194–195.** Weighing the souls of the dead; Book of the Dead of the priest Djed-Khonsou-Iouejankh.